Upland Days

Books by William G. Tapply

FICTION:
The Brady Coyne Novels (17 novels in all)

NONFICTION:
Those Hours Spent Outdoors: Reflections on Hunting and Fishing
Opening Day and Other Neuroses
Home Water Near and Far
Sportsman's Legacy
A Fly-Fishing Life
Bass Bug Fishing
The Elements of Mystery Fiction: Writing a Modern Whodunit

Upland Days

Fifty Years of
Bird Hunting in
New England

William G. Tapply

THE LYONS PRESS

Copyright © 2000 by William G. Tapply

All rights reserved. No part of this book may be reproduced in any manner whatsoever without the express written consent of the publisher, except in the case of brief excerpts in critical reviews and articles. All inquiries should be addressed to: The Lyons Press, 123 West 18 Street, New York, NY 10011

Printed in the United States of America

10 9 8 7 6 5 4 3 2 1

Library of Congress Cataloging-in-Publication Data is available on file.

In memory of
Burton L. Spiller,
my friend and hunting partner

Author's Note

The men, living and dead, whose names are scattered throughout these pages—Dad, Grampa Grouse, Burt Spiller, Keith Wegener, Art Currier, Rick Boyer, Skip Rood, and Marty Connolly—have been my frequent companions in the woods. Without the adventures—and misadventures—we've shared, without their wisdom and good humor and steadfast friendships, I'd have very few stories to tell.

I am indebted to the editors who have encouraged me to write about New England bird hunting and who have published my stories in their magazines, specifically: Duncan Barnes and Slaton White at *Field & Stream*, Ralph Stuart at *Shooting Sportsman*, Jim Babb at *Gray's Sporting Journal*, and Paul Carson at *The Ruffed Grouse Society Magazine*. Many of the stories, reminiscences, and musings in this volume first appeared in those magazines, although I have fiddled with them to the point where they may no longer be recognizable.

When I was a fledgling outdoor writer, I was blessed with the generous advice and encouragement of some savvy old-timers—Frank Woolner, Mark Dilts, and, especially, my father, H. G. "Tap" Tapply. My debt to them is unmeasurable.

I will always be grateful to Nick Lyons for his unwavering support and encouragement, not to mention his inspiration. Outdoor writing in America has no greater friend than Nick.

And, of course, I owe a special debt of gratitude to Vicki Stiefel, my friend, partner, and virtual spouse, for tolerating me and my absentee autumn weekends in general, and for giving me Burt, my Brittany, in particular, and thus for keeping my bird-hunting fires burning bright and hot.

William G. Tapply

September, 2000

Contents

Introduction: Why I Hunt	xi
I—OPENING DAY	**1**
Chapter 1: Partridge Shortenin'	3
Chapter 2: Spiller Country	17
Chapter 3: First Grouse	29
II—WOODCOCK FLIGHTS	**43**
Chapter 4: Little Russet Fellers	45
Chapter 5: The Song of Spring	57
Chapter 6: Woodcock Bottom	63
III—THE DRUMMER	**73**
Chapter 7: Birdy Places	75
Chapter 8: How to Miss Flying Grouse	87
Chapter 9: The Chipmunk Hypothesis	97
Chapter 10: Grudge Grouse	109
IV—OUT OF SEASON	**119**
Chapter 11: Confessions of a Reformed Crow Hunter	121
Chapter 12: Jumping Black Ducks	131
Chapter 13: Virtual Pheasants	143
Chapter 14: Sea Duck Weather	161
Chapter 15: The Year They Opened the Season on Robins	171

V—LAST HUNT	185
Chapter 16: Heartbreak 1963	187
Chapter 17: November Flight	199
Chapter 18: Hunting for Burt	209

Introduction

WHY I HUNT

"How *can* you?"

The first time I heard this question was at a neighborhood cookout about twelve years ago. I'd casually mentioned that I was looking forward to the bird-hunting season, and one of the women wrinkled her nose as if she'd suddenly gotten a whiff of something evil. "How *can* you?" she said.

"What do you mean?" I said, quite innocently. "How can I *what*?"

"Hunt," she said. "Kill."

I felt like asking her how she could eat that cheeseburger or make love to that fat husband of hers or sleep or go to the bathroom or sneeze. Her question struck me as rhetorical, and the answer to it seemed self-evident.

Upland Days

xii

I resisted the impulse to say, "Well, see, you sneak up on some innocent wild creature with sweet brown eyes, and you take your gun, and you aim, and you pull the trigger, and BLAM! That's how. It's easy."

Instead, I recall muttering something inane like, "I dunno. I guess I just enjoy being out in the woods in the fall."

And when she narrowed her eyes and said, "Yes, but—" I made a cowardly escape.

The fact was, I had no ready answer for her. It was a question I'd never felt I needed an answer for. Not everybody hunted, but everybody seemed to at least understand it.

This is no longer the case. Nowadays I get that "How *can* you" question all the time.

And I'm glad I do, because it's forced me to think about it. I suspect I convert no one, and convince few, with my answers. I give my responses earnestly nevertheless. It helps me to keep things clear. . . .

I hunt because my father hunted, and he took me with him, and so we built a bond that I still cherish. I hunt because his father hunted, and his father's father, and all of the fathers in my line and yours, as far back as those fathers who invented spears

Introduction

and axes and recorded their adventures with pictures on the walls of caves.

I hunt because it links me with the boy I used to be and with the young man my father was then.

I hunt because it keeps my passions alive and my memories fresh and my senses alert even as my beard grows gray, and because I fear that if I stopped hunting I would instantly become an old man, and because I believe that as long as I hunt I will remain young.

I hunt because I don't buy futures or sell cars or swing deals, or litigate or prosecute or plea-bargain or negotiate hostile takeovers, but because I am nevertheless, like everyone else, a predator. So I go to the woods where I belong.

I hunt because I love ruffed grouse and woodcock and pheasants and quail and ducks, and because I can imagine no more honorable way for them to die than at the hands of a respectful hunter. For as Thoreau understood, ". . . the hunter is the greatest friend of the animals hunted, not excepting the Humane Society."

I hunt because the goldenrod and milkweed glisten when the early morning October sun melts the frost from the fields, and because native brook trout spawn in hidden autumn streams,

Upland Days

xiv

and because the New England uplands glow crimson and orange and gold in the season of bird hunting.

I hunt because I stumble upon overgrown cellar holes and family graveyards deep in the woods, which reminds me that I'm connected to the farmers who cleared the land and grew their crops and buried their wives and children there, and because I like to believe that I am the first man in a century to stand in those places.

I hunt because Burton Spiller and Gorham Cross hunted; and so did Corey Ford and Ed Zern and Lee Wulff and Harold Blaisdell and Frank Woolner; and because they invited me to hunt with them; and because they were men of my father's generation who treated me like a man when I was a boy; and because they were writers who knew how to tell a story; and because they inspired me to try it for myself.

I hunt because Art Currier and Keith Wegener and Rick Boyer and Skip Rood hunt, and because these are generous and intelligent and witty men, and saner than most. They love and respect the out-of-doors and Nature's creatures, and their friendship has made me a better man than I otherwise would be.

I hunt because the ghosts of beloved companions such as Bucky and Duke and Julie and Megan and Freebie and Waldo

Introduction

prance through the woods, snuffling and tail wagging, making game and pointing, and because Burt, my young Brittany, loves to hunt more than eat, and because hunting dogs make the most tolerant friends. They are smarter in many ways than I am, and they teach me things I wouldn't otherwise understand.

I hunt because I know Thoreau was right: "Fishermen, hunters, woodchoppers, and others, spending their lives in the fields and woods, in a peculiar sense a part of Nature themselves, are often in a more favorable mood for observing her, in the intervals of their pursuits, than philosophers or poets even, who approach her with expectation."

I hunt because I'm convinced, as many anthropologists argue, that prehistoric man was a hunter before he became a farmer, and because this genetic gift remains too powerful in me to resist. I do not need to hunt to eat, but I need to hunt to be fully who I am.

I hunt because it teaches me what it taught our earliest ancestors: cooperation, invention, division of labor, sharing, and interdependence. These are skills that bird hunters must master. Without these derivatives of hunting, our race would still be primitive. As the psychologist Erich Fromm observed, "[Humans] have been genetically programmed through hunt-

Upland Days

xvi

ing behavior: cooperation and sharing. Cooperation between members of the same band was a practical necessity for most hunting societies; so was the sharing of food. Since meat is perishable in most climates except that of the Arctic, it could not be preserved. Luck in hunting was not equally divided among all hunters; hence the practical outcome was that those who had luck today would share their food with those who would be lucky tomorrow. Assuming hunting behavior led to genetic changes, the conclusion would be that modern man has an innate impulse for cooperation and sharing, rather than for killing and cruelty."

I hunt because if I didn't, I would have seen fewer eagles and ospreys, minks and beavers, foxes and bears, antelope and moose, and although I do not hunt these creatures, I do love to enter into their world and spy on them.

I hunt because I love old 20-gauge double-barrel shotguns, and scuffed leather boots with rawhide laces, and canvas vests with a few old breast feathers in their game pockets.

I hunt for the scent of Hoppe's gun oil and camp coffee and wet bird dog and frost-softened, boot-crushed wild apples.

I hunt for the whistle of a woodcock's wings and the sudden explosion of a ruffed grouse's flush, for the tinkle of a dog's bell and the sudden, pulse-quickening silence when he locks on

Introduction

point, for my partner's cry of "Mark!" when he kicks up a bird, for the distant drumming of a grouse, like a balky engine starting up, for the high predatory cry of a red-tail hawk, for the quiet gurgle of a deep-woods trout stream, for the sibilant soughing of the breeze in the pines, for the snoring of my companions in a one-room cabin, and for the soothing patter of an autumn rainstorm on a tin roof.

I hunt because it is never boring or disappointing to be out-of-doors with a purpose, even when no game is spotted, and because taking a walk in the woods without a purpose makes everything that happens feel random and accidental and unearned.

I hunt for the keyed-up conversation, for the laying of plans and the devising of strategies, for the way memory and experience spark imagination and expectation as we drive into the low-angled sunshine on an autumn morning, for the coffee we sip from a dented old Thermos, and for the way the dogs whine and pace on the way to the day's first cover.

And I hunt for the satisfying exhaustion after a long day in the woods, for the new stories that every day of hunting gives us, and for the soft snoring and dream-whimpering and twitching of sleeping dogs on the backseat as we drive home through the darkness.

Upland Days

xviii

I hunt because it reminds me that in Nature there is a food chain where everything eats and is, in turn, eaten; where birth, survival, and reproduction give full meaning to life; where death is ever present, and where the only uncertainty is the time and manner of that death. Hunting reminds me that I am integrated into that cycle, not separate from or above it.

I hunt with a gun, and sometimes I kill. But, as the philosopher José Ortega y Gasset has written, "To the sportsman the death of the game is not what interests him; that is not his purpose. What interests him is everything that he had to do to achieve that death—that is, the hunt. Therefore what was before only a means to an end is now an end in itself. Death is essential because without it there is no authentic hunting: the killing of the animal is the natural end of the hunt and that goal of hunting itself, not of the hunter. The hunter seeks this death because it is no less than the sign of reality for the whole hunting process. . . . One does not hunt in order to kill; on the contrary, one kills in order to have hunted."

I hunt to prevent myself from forgetting that everything I eat once lived, and that it is important to accept responsibility for living at the expense of another life, and that killing is half of the equation of living.

Introduction

I hunt because it is hard and demanding and sometimes dangerous work, and because performing difficult work well gives me pleasure.

And I hunt because it is fun, an intense kind of artistic game, and I like to challenge myself to do it well. As Aldo Leopold wrote, "We seek contacts with nature because we derive pleasure from them. . . . The duck-hunter in his blind and the operatic singer on the stage, despite the disparity of their accoutrements, are doing the same thing. Each is reviving, in play, a drama formerly inherent in daily life. Both are, in the last analysis, esthetic exercises."

I hunt because, in the words of Ortega y Gasset, it gives me "a vacation from the human condition," which, all by itself, is a full and satisfactory reason.

Part I

Opening Day

Can memories be measured by gold? If so, then I am rich indeed. Who can value in gold the worth of the memory of that first grouse, of that first double, or of the day when five grouse got up from a brush pile, one after another while I, armed with a pump gun, missed them all. There are thousands of memory bonds stored in the safe-deposit box of my memory, and each has its coupon of happiness and health attached.
—Burton L. Spiller
DRUMMER IN THE WOODS, 1962

Chapter 1

Partridge Shortenin'

If any word here recalls to old or young some nostalgic remembrance of warm October sun, crisp leaves, incredible shots, frosty mornings, the tangy scent of old apples, the feel of cold gun barrels, a loved dog or elusive birds, I shall be repaid and please remember: any allusions or references to persons or places are purely malicious.

—Grampa Grouse
PARTRIDGE SHORTENIN', 1949

Upland Days

4

The first time I hunted grouse with Keith Wegener, a bird flushed from the edge of a swamp while I was clawing through the limbs of a fallen tree. I screamed "Mark!" as I tried to disentangle myself from a wild grapevine and scramble into position to get a shot. Just as I fired at the flash of gray tailfeathers, my foot caught on a half-buried strand of barbed wire and I fell flat on my face.

I was combing the twigs out of my hair and checking my gun barrels for dents when Keith wandered over. "Well?" he said. "Bring down any feathers?"

"No, dammit," I answered. "The blowdown had me horse-collared and a tripwire snagged me, and besides, that jeesly pat turned out to be a sidewinder. I think I'm gonna grudge him."

Keith frowned at me. "Huh?" he said. "Do you speak English?"

"Sorry," I said. "I forgot you aren't a member of the Grouse Shorteners' Association."

One year, in a predawn kitchen, the grouse shorteners were assembling their gear for a weekend in New Hampshire when the young son of Gorham Cross's partner stumbled downstairs. When the boy's father introduced him to Mr. Cross, the tot rubbed the sleep from his eyes, hitched up his pajamas, and po-

Partridge Shortenin'

5

litely held out his little hand as he'd been taught to do. "Good luck, Mr. Grouse," he mumbled.

Gorham Cross became Mr. Grouse after that, and was delighted to become Grampa Grouse when his first grandchild was born.

He was my father's regular grouse-hunting partner when I might have been that sleepy-eyed boy—and even before—in the 1930s and '40s, and he died just about the time I was old enough to carry a shotgun in the woods. So I became Grampa Grouse's successor. I know Dad was happy to have his son for a partner. But he misses Grampa Grouse to this day.

As much as my partners and I have loved grouse hunting, I'm convinced that no one ever had more fun at it than Grampa. Now, half a century later, Dad still chuckles and shakes his head at Grampa Grouse's sayings and foibles and superstitions and off-kilter wisdom. Sometimes I catch him staring off into space with a soft smile playing on his lips, and I know he's remembering those days he shared with Grampa. That was when New England was dotted with tumbledown cellar holes and intersected with stone walls, when every dirt road led to an abandoned farmyard, when the alders and birch whips grew head-high and the old pastures were studded with juniper clumps and thornapple, when

Upland Days

6

the field edges were thick and brushy, and when ruffed grouse pecked both the gravel beside every roadway and frost-softened Baldwin apples in every overgrown orchard.

In those days, my father's October and November weekends were devoted to bird hunting. Clad in his grouse-hunting costume, Grampa would pull his old Jeep into our driveway before sunup on Saturday morning. Gorham Cross was a respected and well-to-do Boston businessman in his Monday-through-Friday life. But in the woods he wore faded and briar-tattered jeans, a work shirt gone to holes at the elbows, and a shapeless felt hat. In a cold autumn kitchen with a bird-hunting weekend ahead of him, Grampa was as jittery and jangly as the dogs, who skittered their toenails on the linoleum and whined at the back door when they spotted the gun cases and hunting boots piled in the kitchen. They couldn't wait to get going. Neither could Grampa Grouse.

Then the Jeep would appear again after dark on Sunday evening, and Grampa and Dad would unload their birds—always, at least in my memory, a lot of birds.

Grampa Grouse had a round, ruddy, laughing face and a crown of white hair, and I remember my father's affection for his older friend—and his grief the day Grampa died. He was just fifty-nine, way too young.

Partridge Shortenin'

7

Dad's old hunting log records the fact that in my eleventh autumn I began tagging along on some of his weekend hunts with Grampa Grouse. I was too young to carry a gun in the woods, so I dogged my father's footsteps through the thick stuff, and I began to learn what a flushing grouse sounded like and where the birds lurked and how quickly a man had to shoot to hit one.

On the long rides up and back to their New Hampshire grouse country, and on the shorter rides between covers, I sat in the backseat with the dogs. I leaned forward and folded my arms across the top of the front seat so I could listen to the men. They talked grouse talk. Their language was peculiar, decorated with words and phrases that made no sense to me at first.

Luckily for those of us who knew him, Grampa Grouse wrote a book. He called it *Partridge Shortenin'*, "Being," as Grampa expanded his title, "an instructive and irreverent sketch commentary on the psychology, foibles, and footwork of partridge hunters." In 1949 he published it privately in a limited edition of one hundred copies, dedicated it to his wife, "the self-styled Shotgun Widow," and gave copies to his friends. Its pages are unnumbered, reflecting, as Grampa noted, "the fragmentary and haphazard manner in which these yarns have been written and printed."

Upland Days

8

Grampa presented a copy of his book to the young son of his hunting partner, and I have it still. It is, I have been told, treasured among collectors. I have been offered a lot of money for my tattered copy.

For those of us who reread *Partridge Shortenin'* every couple of years, it's a journey back to days of innocence and wonderment that we otherwise might forget. They were my childhood days—and Grampa's, too, because his enthusiasm for upland hunting was childlike right to the end.

Grampa acknowledged and theorized about grouse cycles, but never did he acknowledge the possibility (now, half a century later, a fact) that his beloved covers—Timbertop and Limberlost, Rocky Hill and Binney Hill, Crankcase and Tap's Pines and Clayte Brown's Picker—would be cut down and paved over, or would just evolve into mature forests, and that the day would ever come when broods of partridges would no longer burst from the corners and fly their grooves.

Oh, how Grampa loved grouse, and the men and dogs who hunted them! Every day was an adventure for Grampa, every hunt a war. Grouse were canny adversaries, worthy enemies, and outsmarting them demanded Machiavellian strategies—that failed as often as not, to Grampa's consternation . . . and delight.

Partridge Shortenin'

9

And woe to the fox or hawk who dared to poach on Grampa's beloved grouse. He always carried two loads of high-base Remington 00 buckshot—"varmint shells"—in his shooting vest in case he encountered a grouse predator in the woods.

As much as he loved partridges, though, Grampa loved above all else his hunting partners. "Companionship is the essence of bird shooting," he wrote. "When you get a pal whom you can hunt with, eat and sleep with, drive and endure with for two or three long days, you have a real shooting partner."

If I'd had Grampa's book for those backseat hours, perhaps I'd have been able to follow the men's front-seat conversations more easily. And today, if I were to lend it (which I won't), I wouldn't have to translate myself to my hunting partners.

So here instead, for the uninitiated, is a primer of the grouse-hunting language, as spoken by Grampa Grouse and the other members of the Grouse Shorteners' Association:

Batteries (n.)—Energy (of hunters and dogs); "Let's sit a spell and recharge our batteries."

Battery acid (n.)—What you pour into a steel Stanley thermos; coffee.

Upland Days

10

Been-through (v.)—Previously hunted, usually by rabbit hunters; "Not a single biddie in the whole cover," mourned the Old Master. "Looks like it's been-through." Grampa Grouse believed that the explanation for *all* empty covers was that they'd been-through by rabbit hunters. He refused to acknowledge the possibility that his secret covers could be known to other grouse hunters who might've been-through them or, even worse, that no birds lived in them.

Biddie (n.)—Ruffed grouse (see *Pat*)

Birdy (adj.)—Tense and alert, with wagging tail and snuffling nose (describing the behavior of a bird dog); also, likely to hold grouse (describing the appearance of a cover); "Spotting birdy cover is a matter of observation and experience."

Blowdown (n.)—Fallen trees and limbs (see *Hellhole, Mankiller, Picker, Horsecollar*).

Boiler (n.)—Bladder; ("bust a boiler"—urinate); "All you dogs can bust your boilers," the driver announced.

Bogged down (adj.)—Lethargic; a breakfast of pancakes and sausages can leave a hunter bogged down all morning.

Bull-Briars (n.)—Thorny vegetation with the hostile temperament of an angry bull.

Partridge Shortenin'

Chalking (n.)—The distinctive white splashes left on the ground by woodcock, a sign that woodcock are present or, more likely, that they have recently departed.

Chassis (n.)—Body (referring either to a dog or a person); "Old Dog, shame!" quoth I. "Your chassis is dirty!"

Disagreeable (adj.)—Agreeable; "I'm disagreeable to most anything," chimed the Professor.

Doodle (n.)—Woodcock; short for "timberdoodle."

Guess-What (n.)—The ingredients in sandwiches prepared for hunters by shotgun widows; "a guess-what sandwich."

Groove (adj.)—Predictable; "There's groove birds that fly the same jumps every day till you get them."

Grudge (v.)—To curse; "Grudging is equivalent to putting a ju-ju on a bird. It is a challenge and duly respected by all."

Hellhole (n.)—Thick cover (see *Picker, Mankiller*).

Horse-collared (v.)—Caught in a tangle, usually a combination of blowdowns, briars, and grapevines in a hellhole, mankiller, or picker, that ensnares a hunter and prevents him from snapping off an accurate shot; "We always found ourselves on the wrong side of a tree or horse-collared in bull-briars when a bird got up."

Iron Rations (n.)—Hershey chocolate bar.

Upland Days

12

Jeesly (adj.)—All-purpose malediction, typically applied to imaginary rabbit hunters who have been-through a grouse cover.

Mankiller (n.)—A hellhole or picker where a hunter is sure to get horse-collared.

Mark! (exclam.)—What grouse shorteners scream to alert their partners when a grouse flushes; for those who have been yelling "Mark!" all their lives, it becomes a conditioned reflex; even when hunting alone or just tromping through the woods without a gun, the explosive flush of a grouse causes longtime partridge shorteners to scream "Mark!" the way a dog drools at the sight of his food bowl.

Pants-draggers (n.)—The flotsam and jetsam that hunters carry in their pants pockets; Grampa never entered the woods without ten shotgun shells for birds and two for varmints, a "dollar" pocket watch, iron rations, dog candies, a compass, a Boy Scout knife, a cloth bag for license and money, a waterproof container of matches, tissues in a waxed-paper sandwich bag, and a pencil flashlight.

Parlor (n.)—The prime part of a woodcock cover; a place where woodcock gather to eat worms and exchange gossip about the foibles of partridge and woodcock shorteners.

Pat (n.)—Ruffed grouse; short for "pa'tridge."

Partridge Shortenin'

13

Picker (n.)—Thick cover (see *Hellhole, Mankiller*).

Pickins (n.)—Abundance; e.g., "slim pickins" or "easy pickins."

Popple (n.)—A species of deciduous tree; poplar.

Ravine (n.)—Narrow valley or gulch; rhymes with "grapevine" and pronounced with the accent on the first syllable (RA-vine).

Road Bird (n.)—Grouse that is spotted in the road; "Road birds are exasperatingly tempting. They are harder to harvest, by legitimate methods, than a bird started in cover but are always worth a try, for they may traitorously lead the hunter to other birds or to a new cover."

Seed Bird (n.)—A grouse that hunters don't shoot and that will therefore live to reproduce; excuse for missing an easy shot; "I pulled off him at the last minute. Figured we should leave a seed bird."

Sentinel Bird (n.)—A sly grouse that lurks on the edge of a cover, often in a tree, whose job is to flush loudly at the approach of hunters, alerting all the other grouse in the cover.

Shortenin' (v.)—Shooting and killing; shorteners are those who shoot and kill grouse and thus reduce, or shorten, their numbers.

Shotgun Widow (n.)—Wife of a grouse hunter, esp. in October and November.

Upland Days

14

Sidewinder (n.)—A grouse that flies at a sharp angle to the side, usually up or down a steep slope; often grudged.

Slot Bird (n.)—A grouse whose escape route is a narrow opening in the cover.

Stink Bird (n.)—All species of birds except grouse or woodcock; stink birds mislead inexperienced or overly eager dogs into making game and pointing, to the embarrassment of their owners.

Tripwire (n.)—Any kind of fence wire, often barbed, left lying on or just above the ground for the specific purpose of causing grouse hunters to stumble.

Twig (v.)—Poke with a stick; "When twigged in the eye, ask for time out, or take it, and wait until it clears up."

VWF (abbr.)—Veritable Winter Fairyland; the appearance of a grouse cover after a late-autumn snowstorm.

Wall Bird (n.)—A grouse perched on a stone wall alongside a dirt road; most wall birds are former road birds that moved at the approach of a vehicle.

WGC (abbr.)—Wild Goose Chase; a fruitless hunt; more frequently used in reference to grouse than geese.

Nowadays, it seems, the southern Maine covers that Keith and I treasure—Hippie House and Stick Farm and Rusty Bed-

Partridge Shortenin'

15

spring—come up empty, or close to it, all too often. We rarely spot road birds or wall birds anymore, and few doodles seem to gather in their old favorite parlors.

But at least now, after rambling over dirt roads together for all these years, Keith and I can communicate. Last Saturday, for example, we were feeling pretty bogged down by noontime, so we sat on the ground and leaned our backs against an old stone wall to recharge our batteries. We'd had slim pickins that morning. We'd heard the flush of one sentinel bird, and Burt had bumped a pair of doodles off the sunny side of John's Knoll, and that was it.

"Well," observed Keith between bites of his guess-what sandwich and sips of battery acid, "another WGC. All them pickers must've been-through by a bunch of jeesly rabbit hunters."

Chapter 2

Spiller Country

Three or four times a year I take my old friend's shotgun from my gun cabinet, break it apart, check it for rust, and give it a good cleaning. It's a Parker 20, VH grade, a nice gun—beautiful, in fact—and perhaps modestly valuable. It looks like it's been hunted hard, and it has. Its bluing is worn shiny around the breech and at the ends of the barrels, there are dents in the stock, and the recoil pad is beginning to crumble. I've never bothered to have it appraised. It's not for sale, so why bother, although men who know its provenance have offered me what I'm sure is ten times what a shrewd gunsmith would pay.

I fit it together, snap it to my shoulder, trace the hard flight of a grouse cutting across the wall of my den, and remember all the

Upland Days

18

birds it's shot—and all those I've missed with it. Then I sit back, lay the little Parker on my lap, close my eyes, and indulge myself in a moment of nostalgia for the days when I tromped the uplands with Burt Spiller, and for the days when ruffed grouse prospered in Spiller country.

According to my father's meticulous journals, I hunted with Burton L. Spiller for the first time on November 10, 1951. Well, I didn't actually hunt in those days. I was eleven, too young to carry a gun in the woods. Instead, I followed at my father's heels all day—through briar and alder and mud, uphill and over stone wall and around blowdown. I didn't mind. Grouse hunting in those days was exciting enough, even if you couldn't shoot.

One English setter, two men, and one boy flushed 23 separate grouse that November day in Burt's string of southern New Hampshire covers. Burt, who was sixty-five, walked the field edges and shot one of them with his sleek little Parker. My father dropped three.

Dad's journals suggest that was an average day back then.

We became a regular threesome in the 1955 season. At nine o'clock every Saturday morning, Dad and I would pull up in front of Burt's white frame house in East Rochester. A leg o' mut-

Spiller Country

19

ton gun case, black lunch pail, and a pair of well-oiled boots would already be lined up on the porch, and when Dad tooted the horn, Burt would come out, wave, and lug his gear to the car. "Hi," he always said, grinning. "I've been expecting you. It looks like a wonderful day."

Burton L. Spiller was born on December 21, 1886, the right time; in Portland, Maine, the right place.

The nineteenth-century Maine farmers had opened the land. They moved rocks to clear pastureland and piled them along the edges to make Frost's "good fences." They planted apples—Baldwins and Gravensteins, Northern Spies and Russets and Pippins. Second-growth birch, popple, alder, and hemlock pushed in when the farms were abandoned. Just about the time young Burt was old enough to carry a shotgun into the woods, classic grouse cover was everywhere. No wonder Burt Spiller became a partridge hunter.

He blasted his first grouse off the ground with his father's 10-gauge duck gun when he was seven. "Many, many times I have stood as I stood then," he wrote in "His Majesty, the Grouse," his first published story, "but there has never been another grouse— or another thrill like that one. The kick is still there, as I pre-

Upland Days

20

sume it still is in the old 10-gauge, but—well—we are a little harder around the heart and shoulders than we were then."

A year later the Spillers moved down the seacoast to the little hamlet of Wells, and young Burt's lifelong love affair with the ruffed grouse was sealed. "Other boys of my acquaintance might content themselves with slaying elephants and lions and other inconsequential members of the animal kingdom," he wrote, "but I wanted none of that. . . . Nothing but the lordly pa'tridge would satisfy me."

Eventually Burt bartered his bicycle and his watch for a 16-gauge double and "began to kill grouse regularly on the wing. I used the word 'regularly' advisedly," he wrote, "for the regularity was truly astounding. I shot a bird and killed it. Then I shot at forty-nine more and missed ingloriously. Then I killed another."

When he was a young man, he teamed up briefly with a pair of market hunters, an experience that steeped him in grouse lore and sharpened his wingshooting eye. But eventually he recognized "the difference between a sportsman and that reprehensible thing I was becoming . . . [So] I bought a bird dog and became a sportsman."

In 1911 Burton Spiller married and settled in East Rochester, New Hampshire, where he lived out the rest of his life. He was a

Spiller Country

21

blacksmith and a welder, and during the Great War he built submarines at the Portsmouth Naval Shipyard. He raised and bred prizewinning gladioli. He carved violins and made hunting knives. He hunted—not just grouse and woodcock, but ducks and deer, too—and he fished for brook trout and landlocked salmon.

And although he was pretty much self-educated, he began to write, working nights on his old Oliver typewriter. He sold "His Majesty, the Grouse" to *Field & Stream* in 1931. It was the first of fifty-three Spiller stories that magazine would print. The last was "Grouse Oddities," in 1967, when Burt was eighty-one.

Between 1935 and 1938 the Derrydale Press published a Spiller book a year—all numbered, deluxe editions limited to 950 copies. First came the classic *Grouse Feathers*, then *Thoroughbred*, and *Firelight*, and *More Grouse Feathers*. All have been reprinted one time or another. Those original Derrydales are treasures.

Around that time, someone dubbed Burt "the poet laureate of the ruffed grouse." The name stuck, as it should have.

In 1962 *Drummer in the Woods*, a collection of previously published grouse stories (mostly from *Field & Stream*), appeared. Burt also wrote a boys' adventure yarn called *Northland Cast-*

Upland Days

22

aways, and in 1974, the year after he died, *Fishin' Around,* a collection of his low-key fishing stories, appeared.

I guess at one time or another, while the two of us were eating my mother's applesauce cake by a New Hampshire brook or bouncing over a dirt road between covers or trudging side by side down an overgrown tote road, Burt told me most of his stories. Whenever I reread a couple of them, as I do every time I take out the old Parker, I can hear Burt's soft voice, see the twinkle in his eye, and feel his finger poking my arm for emphasis.

In 1955, when I began hunting regularly with him, Burt was already sixty-nine years old. He was a small, wiry, soft-spoken man, old enough to be my father's father. I called him "Mr. Spiller," as I'd been taught to do. But on the first morning of our first hunt he put his hand on my shoulder and said, "Burt, please. Call me Burt. When a grouse gets up, you can't go yelling 'Mark! Mr. Spiller,' now, can you?"

I never heard him raise his voice, curse even mildly, or criticize or poke fun at any man or dog. He was a devout church-going family man who did not hunt on Sundays, even though it was legal in New Hampshire, or drink alcohol, but he was neither pious nor self-righteous.

Spiller Country

23

A good joke, for Burt, was a joke on himself. His favorite stories were about the grouse that outsmarted him and the times he got lost in the woods.

He wore an old-fashioned hearing aid, the kind that plugged into his ear with wires running to the battery in his pocket. "I can hear pretty well," he told me cheerfully, "but sometimes I have trouble picking up the direction." It had to have been a terrible handicap for a grouse hunter, and it probably accounted for the fact that even in those years when partridge were bountiful in his covers, many a day passed when Burt never fired his gun.

When he saw a bird, though, his swing was as silky as I guessed it had been fifty years earlier. Once he and I were trudging side by side up the old Tripwire woods road on our way back to the car. Our guns dangled at our sides, and we were talking and admiring the way the October sunlight filtered through the golden foliage of the beeches that bordered the roadway and arched overhead. Dad and the dog were working their way along parallel to us, somewhere far off to the left.

Suddenly Dad yelled, "Mark! Your way!"

A moment later a grouse crashed through the leaves and rocketed across the narrow road in front of us. It didn't make it. Burt's Parker spoke once, and the bird cartwheeled to the ground.

Upland Days

24

It was a spectacular shot.

Burt picked up the stone-dead partridge and stroked its neck feathers. Then he looked up at me. He shook his head and smiled apologetically. "Sorry," he said. "I should have let you take him."

He knew, of course, that the odds of my shooting that grouse were exactly the same as his own when he'd been my age: about one in fifty. But that was Burt.

I was young and eager, and I tended to measure the success of a day's hunting by the heft of my game pocket. I learned how to hit flying grouse the old-fashioned way—by shooting often and relying on the law of averages—and as much as I missed, and as much as I expected to miss, I still tended to kick stumps and grumble and sulk when it kept happening.

Burt used to tell me, "Just keep shootin'. You can't hit anything if you don't shoot. And always remember: Every time you hit a flying grouse is a good shot."

I noticed that he never grumbled or sulked when he missed, although, to be accurate, he didn't seem to miss very often. Even on those days when birds were scarce or it rained or the dog behaved poorly or nobody got any shots, Burt always had fun. Afterward, when we dropped him off at his house, he always smiled and said the same thing: "A wonderful hunt. See you next week."

Spiller Country

25

Gradually I learned to say the same thing at the end of every day—"A wonderful hunt"—and *mean* it. Burt taught me that.

He was moving a lot slower by 1964, and although he still wore the old hearing aid, he didn't seem to pick up sounds as well. Burt was seventy-eight that year. He still greeted us the same way when we picked him up in the morning: "Hi. I've been expecting you. It looks like a wonderful day."

On the second weekend of the season, after we laced on our boots at our Bullring cover for the day's first hunt, Burt said, "Uh, Bill? Can I heft your gun?"

I handed him my cheap Savage single-shot.

He threw it to his shoulder. "Comes up nice," he said. "Mind if I try it?"

"Sure," I said, though I couldn't understand why he'd want to.

"Here," he said. "You better take mine." He handed me his slick little Parker.

I carried Burt's gun through the Bullring, and he carried mine. I recall missing a couple of woodcock with it. Burt, straggling along the fringes of the cover, had no shots.

At our next stop, Burt picked up the Savage. "Never got to fire it back there," he said. "Mind if I try it again?"

Upland Days

26

And so Burt lugged my gun around that day while I carried his Parker, and Dad's journal reports that I ended up shooting a woodcock, while Burt never dirtied the barrel of that Savage.

When we dropped him off, he said, "Why don't you hang on to that gun if you want to."

"Well, sure," I stammered. "I mean, I'd love to."

He smiled and waved. "A wonderful hunt, wasn't it?"

The next week when we stopped for Burt, it was my Savage that stood on his porch alongside his lunch pail and boots, and he carried it all day while I toted the Parker. And nothing was ever again said about it. We had swapped guns, and Burt had managed to accomplish it his own way, without ceremony. He never even gave me the chance to properly thank him.

I know for certain that Burton Spiller shot only one more grouse in his life, and it happened a couple of weeks after we'd exchanged guns. He was following a field edge while Dad and I were slogging through the thick stuff, and a bird flushed wild and headed in Burt's direction. Dad screamed, "Mark! Burt!" and I could hear the frustration in his voice, knowing that Burt probably couldn't hear him and wouldn't hear or see the bird.

But a moment later, from far off to our right, came a single shot.

Spiller Country

27

We hooked over to the field and emerged behind Burt. He was trudging slowly up the slope, my gun over his right shoulder and a grouse hanging by its legs from his left hand.

Burt Spiller shot his last partridge with my gun.

The following Saturday, October 31, 1964, sometime in the morning Burt fell. He never complained—didn't even tell us when it happened—but by the middle of the afternoon he had to call it quits.

He was still hurting the next week and the week after, and then the season was over.

Burt Spiller had hunted grouse for the last time.

During the next decade, Dad and I visited him periodically. He always had a smile and wanted to hear about our hunting trips.

He told us he had no desire to hunt again. He'd had a lifetime of it, and he cherished all the memories.

He continued to write stories and raise gladioli right up to his death on May 26, 1973.

A few months later, the old Savage came back to me with Burt's instruction: "For Bill's son."

Upland Days

28

Dad and I continued to hunt Spiller country for the next several seasons. Then one October we found that a power line had been cut right through the heart of Schoolhouse. The next winter, Bullring became a highway cloverleaf; then a Stop & Shop parking lot took the upper end of Tap's Corner. A couple of years later, the dirt road to The Old Hotel got paved over, and pastel-colored ranch houses sprouted up along both sides.

Burt's covers, those that remained, changed, too. Mankiller and Tripwire just didn't look birdy anymore. The hillsides that had once sprouted thick with juniper and birch whips and head-high alders grew into mature pine-and-hardwood forests, and after a while we stopped hunting Spiller country altogether.

It was never the same anyway. It always seemed as if we'd forgotten the most important stop of all—at the white frame house in East Rochester, where Burt would come to his door on a Saturday morning, grin and wave, lug his gear to the car, and say, "Hi. I've been expecting you. It looks like a wonderful day."

Chapter 3

First Grouse

"Children," my father liked to say, "should be seen and not heard."

It was something I tried hard to be good at. I made a special point of being seen, because I didn't want to be overlooked. So when my father rose before dawn on those Saturday mornings in October and November, I got up, too. I helped lug the gear up from the cellar and set it out on the back porch: the leg o' mutton shotgun case, my father's big duffel bag, the wicker lunch basket, and the canvas bag that held boxes of shells, topographic maps, the dog's belled collar, cans of horsemeat, and rags pungent with Hoppe's.

Upland Days

30

In the kitchen, my father worked over the black skillet where the bacon sizzled and spat. When his partner arrived, I sat with the men at the cramped table watching the suburban sky brighten over the backyard. My father called him Grampa, and I was expected to, also. Grampa Grouse was white-haired, rosy-cheeked, and jolly, always bubbling with enthusiasm—my vision of Santa Claus—and he loved to tell extravagant stories about partridge and the dogs and men who hunted them.

I ate with the men while the dogs waited under the table. Grampa Grouse slipped crusts of toast and strips of bacon to them, and when the men pushed back their chairs and lit their pipes, the dogs' tails began to thump against the floor. Then they uncurled themselves and scratched and skidded across the linoleum to the back door and began to whine and bump their noses against it.

That, in turn, signaled the men to get up from the table. "The dogs need to bust their boilers," Grampa Grouse would say, and he'd let them into the backyard. My father would kiss my mother and clap my shoulder. And then the two men would leave.

On Sunday night I would meet them at Grampa Grouse's wagon when it pulled into the driveway. I'd help my father lug in

First Grouse

the gear and the dead birds, and then I'd watch while he cleaned them at the kitchen sink. My job was to swab out the barrels of my father's shotgun and rub it down with an oily rag. I performed this important job with care. I knew my father would peer through the barrels and look for fingerprints on the metal, and I understood that cleaning a shotgun properly was one step toward earning the right to shoot it.

I didn't really mind having been left behind. My day would come. I knew that.

I imagined it would be a dramatic moment, like getting married or having my first drink of whiskey. There would be a speech about the serious nature of firearms and adult responsibility and the honored ceremonies of grouse hunting, and how being seen and not heard was important for men as well as boys.

When it actually happened, the moment could have almost slipped past without being noticed. One Friday evening in the October after I turned eleven, my father looked up from his newspaper and said, "Want to come with us tomorrow?"

I rode in the backseat for the two-hour drive into New Hampshire. My father and Grampa Grouse talked about business and politics and foreign policy, about men and bird dogs who had died, subjects not selected for my interest, but not censored

Upland Days

32

because I was in the backseat, either. They included me, I understood, by not excluding me.

I was not allowed to carry a gun on this, my first grouse hunt. "Walk directly behind me," my father instructed me while we laced on our boots at the first cover. "Stay close to me, and keep your eyes and ears open. When a bird flushes, fall flat to the ground. If you can't do that, you'll have to stay in the car."

Grouse covers, I quickly learned, were thick, hostile places, nothing like the Aden Lassell Ripley watercolors that hung in my father's den. Grouse covers were hilly, rocky, brushy, muddy hellholes where hunters had to wade through juniper clumps and claw through briar patches and clamber over blowdowns. I struggled to keep up. Sometimes saplings snapped back against my face and made my eyes water.

Once my feet got tangled and I fell. Before I could scramble to my feet, my father stopped and looked back at me. "You've got to keep up," he said.

"I tripped," I said. "It's hard walking."

"You can go back to the car if you want."

"I'm okay."

The first time a grouse flushed, I watched my father's gun snap up and shoot into the thick autumn foliage. The gun seemed to

First Grouse

33

react on its own, independent of the man who carried it. I never saw the bird. I only heard the sudden, explosive whirr.

"Well?" called Grampa Grouse from somewhere off to the right.

"Nope," called my father. "Dog busted him."

Then he turned and looked at me. I was standing there right behind him. "I told you to fall to the ground when a bird gets up," he said.

"I heard the noise," I said. "I didn't know . . ."

"That was a grouse. That's the noise they make when they flush. You've got to go to the ground."

"Okay," I said. "I understand."

I learned that grouse hunting involved miles of hard walking, a great deal of yelling at the dogs, frequent shooting, and not much killing.

The day was warm and I soon grew tired. The part I liked best was returning to Grampa's wagon after each cover. There the men would pour coffee for me from a big steel thermos. The coffee was cut with milk and sweetened with sugar. I had never tasted coffee before that day. It wasn't whiskey, but drinking coffee for the first time nevertheless seemed important.

Upland Days

34

Many grouse flushed that morning, and I quickly learned to fall to the ground at the sound. When my father finally shot one, he turned and said, "Did you see that?"

"Of course not," I said. "I was lying on the ground."

He smiled.

We ate lunch by a brook in the woods. Thick corned-beef-and-cheese sandwiches made with slices of bread my mother had baked. Big wedges of applesauce cake, my mother's secret recipe. More sweet coffee. I grew drowsy. My legs ached.

After a while, Grampa Grouse unfolded himself, stood up, and stretched. "Better get a move on," he said. "Don't want to get all bogged down."

It grew cloudy and cooler in the afternoon. A soft rain began to sift down from the gray sky, and the woods were silent except for the tinkle of the dogs' bells and the occasional whistles that my father exchanged with Grampa Grouse. My pants soaked up rainwater from the brush. I found myself stumbling. I hoped it would be over soon. I plodded along behind my father, my eyes on the ground so I wouldn't trip and fall again.

We were moving through an old apple orchard that grew thick with juniper and thornapple and popple and alder. A blanket of small, hard Baldwin apples carpeted the ground under the trees.

First Grouse

35

They cracked under my boots. The woods smelled sweet with their ripe aroma.

Suddenly my father stopped. "Look!" he hissed.

I peered along his pointing arm and saw the big bird perched on the lowest limb of a gaunt old apple tree. One of the dogs stood directly underneath, looking up. The grouse craned its neck, peering down at the dog.

My father pressed his shotgun into my hands. "Shoot him," he said.

I had fired my father's shotgun just once in my life. I'd shot it at a rusty old oil drum. The oil drum had disintegrated. My father had said, "Good shot," but I understood it had nothing to do with marksmanship. That had been a lesson about the power of shotguns.

I pressed the gun against my shoulder, aimed it at the grouse in the apple tree, and tugged at the trigger. Nothing happened.

"The safety," my father whispered. "Quick."

I remembered. I thumbed off the safety, set the bird over the barrels, and pulled the trigger. The gun sounded louder than I remembered from shooting at the oil drum. The grouse fell from the tree.

"Hey!" my father said. "You got him. Good shot."

Upland Days

36

The dog came trotting in with the dead grouse in his mouth. My father took it from the dog, stroked the bird's feathers, then handed it to me. "Your first grouse," he said. "Congratulations."

I carried the grouse by its feet through the rest of the cover. When we got back to Grampa Grouse's wagon, my father took a picture of me. Grampa punched my shoulder and called me Nimrod.

The men tried to act as if my first grouse was a big triumph, but I understood that hitting a sitting grouse with a shotgun was no great feat. No different from shooting an oil drum, really. Something any boy could do. I also understood, because I'd been paying attention that day, that the men shot only at flying grouse.

Being seen but not heard, of course, I did not share this understanding with my father and Grampa Grouse.

After that day, I accompanied my father almost every autumn weekend, and when I turned thirteen, my father gave me my own shotgun, a single-barrel Savage 20-gauge with a thumb safety.

Being seen and not heard, I had come to realize, enabled me to learn a great deal. I absorbed what the men said—from the

First Grouse

backseat and in grouse covers and while eating lunch alongside brooks and in hotel dining rooms. I watched what the dogs did, and the paths my father took through the woods, and I noticed the kinds of places where grouse were normally found.

Now, carrying my own shotgun and walking my own routes through covers, I found I had a good instinct for grouse. My father, Grampa Grouse, and I worked as a team, pinching birds between us so that one or the other of us would get a good shot.

There were a lot of grouse in the New England woods in those days, and I had my share of chances. My father had told me that having a single-shot gun would make me a better marksman, but it didn't work out that way. I had quick reflexes, and soon my Savage was coming to my shoulder and my thumb was flicking off the safety and I was pulling the trigger without any conscious thought. I shot often. I took crossing shots and straightaway shots and odd-angled shots at flying grouse. I learned to shoot through the leaves where I thought a grouse might be headed, and sometimes I shot at the sound of the flush when all I saw was a quick blur.

I never once hit a flying grouse.

"Keep shooting," my father counseled. "You can't hit what you don't shoot at. It'll happen. The good old law of averages, right?"

Upland Days

38

A couple of times I broke my private vow and shot a grouse out of a tree or off a stone wall. I did it out of anger and frustration at my own incompetence, and even when my father congratulated me on bagging a bird, I found that it gave me no satisfaction whatsoever. Men, I knew, did not shoot sitting grouse.

For the entire season of my thirteenth year and most of the next one, too, I kept my wingshooting streak alive. I shot often and missed every time.

When we hunted with other men, neither my father nor I mentioned my perfect record, the fact that I had never once downed a flying grouse. Since everybody missed grouse far more often than they hit them, nobody except my father knew my secret.

I understood that shooting grouse out of the air was not really the main point of grouse hunting. I liked figuring out where a grouse might be, sneaking up on it, planning how I'd get a shot when it flushed, or if I didn't, how one of the other men would. I liked watching the dogs work. I liked the New England woods in the fall, the way the melting frost glistened on the goldenrod early in the morning and the way Baldwin apples smelled when the ground was blanketed with them. I liked riding in the backseat with the dogs, listening to the men talk, being seen and not heard.

First Grouse

But I had never shot a flying grouse. That single fact separated me from the men. Shooting a few from trees or stone walls didn't count. Boys did that, not men.

On the final weekend of that year's grouse season, my father and I traveled to a new area. We hunted with three old friends of his, men I had never met.

These men included me in their conversations and treated me like a man. They had not known me when I plodded through grouse covers in my father's footsteps. They had not witnessed my first grouse, shot out of a tree. They didn't know that I had never shot a grouse on the wing. I spoke when spoken to, and otherwise continued to be seen and not heard.

We found very few grouse on Saturday. Two of the men missed hasty shots. I never saw a feather, never even had a chance to shoot and miss.

Sunday, the last day of the season, was one of those dark, bitter, late-November New England days. Winter was in the air. Heavy clouds hung over the leafless woods, and now and then a few hard kernels of snow spit down from the sky. We hunted all morning and never flushed a grouse. At lunch the men talked about calling it a season and getting an early start for home.

Upland Days

40

But one of them said he had a secret cover we ought to try first, and the others agreed, although I noticed their lack of enthusiasm.

The birdy part of the cover lay at the end of a long tote road that twisted down a hill through a mixture of pine and poplar. The men and I trudged along with our shotguns at our sides while the dogs, who seemed to have lost their enthusiasm, too, snuffled along ahead of us.

Suddenly the man in front stopped and raised his hand. "We got a point," he whispered.

I looked, and there, under an apple tree at the foot of the hill, I saw the dog stretched out.

"There she is!" hissed the man a moment later, and I saw her, too—a grouse pecking fallen apples about fifteen feet from the dog's nose.

We stood there in the path for a minute, just watching, the dog staunch on point, the grouse oblivious, pecking apples, taking a step, bending to take another peck.

Then one of the men touched my shoulder and said, "You take her."

I caught my father's eye. He nodded. So I stepped forward, gripping my Savage single-shot at port arms, and approached the place where the dog was still on point.

First Grouse

41

The grouse had wandered into the thick undergrowth, and for a minute I couldn't see her. Then I did. She had stopped and twisted her neck around to look directly at me. I stood there, staring back into her intelligent, glittery eyes.

From behind me, one of the men said, "Go ahead. Shoot her. Quick, before she flies."

I raised my gun to my shoulder and aimed at the bird. The grouse kept peering at me.

Then I lowered my gun. I couldn't do it. Shooting this grouse on the ground would prove nothing, and I felt that I had something I needed to prove.

Boys, I thought, shoot grouse on the ground. Men only shoot them when they're flying.

I'd miss, of course. I always did. So what? Better to miss like a man than kill a grouse like a boy.

Then the grouse ducked her head, scuttled deeper into the brush, and disappeared from sight. I stepped forward, paused, then took another step.

The grouse exploded, practically from under my feet. She rose, then suddenly angled toward the left. I have no memory of my gun coming up, my thumb flicking off the safety, my finger pulling the trigger.

Upland Days

42

But I heard the muffled thump of the bird hitting the ground and the quick flurry of wingbeats, and then I heard the men behind me shouting.

A moment later the dog brought the grouse to me. I took her in my hand, smoothed her feathers, tucked her into the pocket in the back of my vest, and walked back to where the men were standing. I was surprised that I felt no particular elation.

"Good shot," said one of the men. "Nice goin'," said another, and I caught the tone I'd hoped for in their voices: It had been a good shot, not a spectacular one, they were saying. It was a shot that grouse hunters often miss but sometimes make, and I had done well.

There was no exaggerated celebration, as there might have been had they known that I had never before shot a grouse out of the air, and that was exactly the way I wanted it.

I glanced at my father, begging him with my eyes not to reveal my secret. My father nodded once, then turned to the other men. "So," he said, "is the rest of this cover worth hunting?"

Part II

Woodcock Flights

Year by year the situation became worse. Woodcock hunters became morose, blaming the bird scarcity on indiscriminate shooting in the Gulf States and Cuba, and considered writing their Congressmen about it. One Maine man became so distraught that he even threatened to vote the Democratic ticket in the next election.
—Burton L. Spiller
DRUMMER IN THE WOODS, 1962

Chapter 4

Little Russet Fellers

Freebie's tail blurred as she snuffled and snorted a slow zigzag through the alders. She stopped abruptly, poised with her weight canted precariously forward.

"We got a point," I called to Keith on my right flank.

The Stick Farm, our morning leg-stretcher, had been empty. John's Knoll, the sun-drenched slope where a mix of poplar, pine, and apple grew, was also empty. Arnold's Pasture, muck-bottomed and alder-studded, fertilized and trampled by the old farmer's dairy cows—empty. We had startled some spawn-minded native brookies from a rocky pool in the little rill that meandered behind the Hippie House. But no woodcock.

Upland Days

46

There didn't seem to be a woodcock in the entire state of Maine.

For the previous several years I'd been studying reports and talking with biologists and game wardens and hunters. Woodcock were in trouble, everyone agreed.

I'd seen the evidence myself, but I'd fooled myself into discounting it. I'd blamed the dog, figured we'd been looking in the wrong places or had mistimed the flights. I didn't want to believe it. But on this day, the second Saturday of October, usually prime time, I believed it. Woodcock were definitely in trouble.

I eased myself forward. "Easy, Freeb," I murmured. "Good girl. Steady, now." She rolled her eyes back at me. I stepped in front of her.

The round little bird rose with its characteristic twitter. Slow motion, angling sharply upward to the top of the alders, pausing there as if it might lose its struggle against gravity, then slanting to its left, quartering away.

My shotgun had mounted itself, and the bird was a lollipop. An easy shot. A gimme.

"Bang!" I said.

The woodcock continued to fly.

Little Russet Fellers

47

"Bang!" I repeated. Then I lowered my gun and watched it glide into the alder swamp beyond the field.

Keith came over. "What was it?"

"Woodcock."

"About time. Freebie bust it?"

"Nope. She did good."

"You didn't shoot," said Keith.

"Safety stuck," I lied.

"Get a line on it?"

"No." Another lie.

He shrugged. "No harm. One woodcock doesn't make much of a meal."

I was introduced to woodcock one October Saturday nearly fifty years ago. A Nor'easter had blown in overnight, driving before it sheets of hard rain that ripped the leaves from the maples behind our suburban Massachusetts house. By morning the wind had fallen, but the rain continued hard, steady, and cold. My father, who rarely behaved sensibly when it came to his weekend hunting excursions to New Hampshire, had sensibly canceled his plans.

Upland Days

48

He wandered through the house for a while, mumbling to himself. He went down to the cellar and frowned at the stack of storm windows that would soon need to be hung. Then he went out to the car, drove down to the hardware store, and returned an hour later, empty-handed.

Around noon he appeared in the kitchen wearing his foul-weather gear and lugging his shotgun. Bing, our young Brittany, scrambled from beneath the kitchen table, his claws scratching and skidding on the linoleum, and began to prod the back door with his nose.

"You're going hunting, aren't you?" said my mother.

"Yep," said Dad.

"Oh, brother." She put a hand over her mouth to hide her smile.

"Want to come?" my father asked me.

"It's raining."

"Sure. Coming?"

"You bet," I said.

We drove to Lincoln, about ten minutes from our house. A road now cuts through the pine grove near where we parked that day, and a pod of cedar-sheathed contemporary homes presently snug-

Little Russet Fellers

49

gles against the hillside where we hunted. But back then it was just a big old rolling pasture grown head-high in poplar and birch.

I was twelve, and for me, hunting did not include carrying a gun. So I tracked behind Bing and my father as well as my short legs would allow. The hard rain clattered on the hood of my oilskin poncho. My feet were soaked. Head down, I trudged after them, intent on keeping up, not at all sure what this hunting was all about.

Suddenly he stopped. "Point," he hissed.

Bing was stretched out, motionless, his head curved awkwardly sideways, his stubby little tail rigid. My father walked past him, and then I heard an odd whistle, glimpsed a brown ball of feathers rising from the ground, saw my father's shotgun move to his shoulder, noted the way the raindrops bounced off the barrels, heard a single report, and watched the bird plummet to the ground. Bing bounded forward and returned an instant later with a dead bird in his mouth.

My father took it from him, patted his head, then turned and handed the bird to me.

I held it in both hands. It weighed less than I expected. I smoothed its wet feathers with my fingers. Two boggled eyes

Upland Days

50

were perched oddly at the top of its head. It had a long slender beak. It looked, I thought, more like a big insect than a bird.

"It's a woodcock," said Dad quietly. "A lovely little bird. The beak is for catching worms underground. He can move it around even after it's in the earth. The eyes are placed up there so he can watch for danger while probing for worms. His ears are in front of his eyes so he can hear the worms moving underground, and his brain is upside down. I don't know why that is."

I handed the woodcock back to Dad. He hefted it gently in the palm of his hand for a moment before dropping it into his game pocket. "It's kind of a shame to shoot them," he said. "Wish we could put them back, like trout."

Bing pointed three more times in the next hour. Dad shot three more times. Bing trotted in with a dead woodcock in his mouth three more times. Then my father broke his shotgun and we headed back to the car.

Four shots in a little more than an hour. Two brace of woodcock. It seemed like a very simple sport.

The following Monday the sun was shining. When I got home from school, Dad was waiting for me. "Want to go hunting?" he said.

I sure did.

Little Russet Fellers

We drove back to Lincoln, parked in the same place we had on Saturday, and trekked to the hillside. And that afternoon I learned my first truth about woodcock. We hunted for three hours. We flushed nothing.

"You must've shot them all," I said afterward.

"Doubt it," Dad said.

"Then where are all the woodcock?"

He shrugged, and when he gave me his answer, it was as if he were equating the comings and goings of woodcock with good fortune, or with the mysteries of life itself. "They migrate," he said.

Years later I met a grizzled game warden beside a dirt road in southern Vermont. After showing him my license and my empty game pocket, and having no false pride on the subject, I asked him if he knew how I might find a local woodcock. He tilted his head and chewed his cigar, as if he were deciding on the wisdom of sharing his hard-earned lore with an out-of-stater.

Then he removed his cigar from his mouth and pointed the wet end at me. "Woodcock," he said solemnly, "are where you find 'em."

I never did decide whether he was telling me everything he knew on the subject—that woodcock, like all good things, were

Upland Days

52

here today and gone tomorrow, and you should always count your blessings—or whether he was just being evasive.

Burt Spiller called them "little russet fellers." Woodcock were by-products of grouse hunts during the first few years I hunted with Burt and my father. Grouse were abundant in those days. Twenty-five or thirty starts were typical. We often found whole broods. The cover was prime: gnarled old Baldwins that left blankets of rotting fruit underfoot, plenty of wild grape, stands of second-growth birch and poplar, pine and hemlock edges, abandoned pastureland grown to clumps of saplings and juniper.

Sometimes the odd woodcock spiraled up from where a grouse ought to have been, and once in a while a flight settled overnight into one of our grouse covers. Then twelve or fifteen woodcock might blunder up from the ground in an area the size of a football field. Woodcock were a diversion in those days, and Dad and Burt often shot limits. They rarely seemed to miss.

Shooting a grouse, I concluded, was a triumph.

But shooting a woodcock was easy, and a cause for vague regret.

The first day I was allowed to carry a gun in the woods, I killed the first two woodcock I shot at. It *did* seem easy, and I assumed that the triumph I felt would eventually be superseded by regret.

Little Russet Fellers

For the rest of that day I proceeded to empty a box of shells at twisting, diving, and darting woodcock without ruffling one more feather. This taught me another lesson about woodcock hunting.

I am always surprised to realize how few people have ever seen, or even heard of, woodcock. I guess I shouldn't be. They are mysterious, wraithlike, diffident creatures. They travel on the dark of the moon, and during the day they hide in places where sensible humans rarely set foot. It's hardly surprising that good remaining woodcock cover is rapidly going over to suburban development, shopping malls, and interstate highways. Prime woodcock habitat isn't good for much except harboring woodcock, and there seem to be too few of us who love the little russet fellers to raise an effective complaint against the forces of "progress."

Most woodcock habitat, of course, has succumbed to a different kind of progress. Those pastures and hillsides where head-high saplings once grew have matured into forests, devoid of the thick understory that woodcock need for survival, and I don't expect an army of tough Yankee farmers will ever again come along to clear the New England countryside for dairy pastures and bean fields.

# Upland Days

54

Grouse became scarcer during those years I hunted with Dad and Burt Spiller. Increasingly we looked for woodcock cover. We drove the back roads, scouting for alder-rimmed streambeds, birch or poplar hillsides, clumpy old pasturelands.

Worms, I learned, are the woodcock's primary food. Good worm cover is good woodcock cover.

Burt taught me to recognize the woodcock's chalk-colored splashings on the ground. Wet chalkings meant woodcock were nearby. Dried-up chalkings meant they had departed.

Naturally, more often than not, the chalkings we found were dried up.

Once Dad knelt and pointed to a series of tiny punctures in the black mucky earth. "Drill holes," he said. "Woodcock have been here."

Mossy ground is acidic ground, I understood. It's no good for worms. Same with pine needles. And if it's too grassy, the birds can't maneuver their beaks down to where the worms live.

Migrating woodcock, as opposed to the "natives" that stopped in our New England covers to raise their young and spend the summer, could not be counted on to act according to form. We sometimes found flight birds in pine woods and open grassy

Little Russet Fellers

55

fields. Once we spotted a dozen of them probing for worms on an unused baseball infield.

Eventually I devised my own corollary to one of my early lessons: Woodcock are not where you don't find them.

Back in Keith's truck, we shared the lukewarm dregs of the day's coffee. Freebie curled on the backseat, bored and tired from a day virtually devoid of heady bird smells.

"Your safety didn't really stick, did it?" asked Keith.

"What are you talking about?"

"I heard you say something when that woodcock flushed. Didn't sound like cussing."

"I wasn't cussing."

"It sounded like you said 'bang-bang.' "

I shrugged. "That's what I said."

Keith stared out the window at the darkening woods. "Correct me if I'm wrong," he said. "But I thought we were hunting."

I nodded. "We are."

"We got up at six in the morning, drove two and a half hours, and plodded untold sweating, bleeding miles through fen and bog and blowdown, up mountain and down ravine, getting twigged in the eyes and thorned on the hands. For what?"

Upland Days

56

"Woodcock. We're woodcock hunting."

"Correct. And what happened when we finally found one?"

"I didn't shoot it."

"You didn't even shoot *at* it," he said, correcting me. "Wanna tell me why?"

"Sure," I said. "I was putting it back. Like a trout."

Chapter 5

The Song of Spring

According to the Seneca Indians, after the Maker finished creating all the creatures of the Earth, He looked around and realized He had some leftover parts. There was a small pile of feathers—not big flashy ones, for those had been taken by the glamorous species He had already created, but drab, earth-toned grays and browns. There was a head, but the brain was upside down, and the ears were misplaced in front of boggled eyes, and the beak was disproportionately long. He found a chunky little body and stubby legs and sturdy but graceless wings. It was an ill-matched assortment of parts, but because the Maker hated to waste anything, He put them all together and called it a woodcock.

Upland Days

The Maker realized he'd shortchanged the little bird in the body parts department, so He compensated by giving the woodcock an extra amount of courage, stamina, wisdom, and mystery.

When humans decided to bestow upon the woodcock a proper Greek name, they called him *Philohela minor*, which means Little Sun Lover—a profound misnomer. Woodcock migrate by night and stick close to thick cover during the day.

Early observers, noticing how woodcock kept plunging those long prehensile beaks into the soft ground, surmised that they ate mud. Even today, some people call them "bog suckers" or "mudsuckers" or, because of their erratic nocturnal flights, "mudbats." They also go by regional nicknames: wood snipe, mud snipe, timberdoodle. Frank Woolner, who wrote lovingly of woodcock, proposed "whistledoodle," but it didn't stick.

Sometime around the middle of March, my woodcock return home to New England from their winter sojourns in places as far south as Louisiana. They've been flying northward for several weeks, impelled by—by what? By the changing angle of the sun, the sniff of warming air, a new moon phase, the northward shift of prevailing winds? By Nature's most powerful urge of all, the instinct to procreate?

The Song of Spring

It's probably a combination of all of these things, fine-tuned over countless generations and firmly embedded in woodcock DNA to ensure the survival of their species.

One thing is certain: The family urge is upon them. They fly by night, rest by day, and hardly feed at all, beating relentlessly northward to the precise field or hillside where they were born. Their hormones fuel their single-minded purpose. The males stake out their territory, and the females wait nearby to be courted. It's called the "singing ground."

Biologists have yet to find a more reliable method for taking their annual American woodcock census than by counting the birds they hear singing in the evenings during their mating season and comparing the numbers with those of previous years.

For me, spying on courting woodcocks has always been a springtime ritual. As much as cutting pussy willows, watching the ice break up in my pond, spotting my first robin, seeing my first mayfly, or casting to my first trout of the season, hearing my year's first woodcock song marks the certain end of a long New England winter.

The American woodcock is a peculiar, private, funny-looking, and altogether lovable little bird. Aside from a small breed of peculiar, private, funny-looking, and generally lovable sportsmen

Upland Days

60

who hunt them with pointing dogs and double-barrel shotguns, few people are aware of the woodcock or would recognize one if they saw it, even though they are not uncommon in their two flyways along the Mississippi River and the Atlantic coast. Woodcock lurk in dark alder tangles or remote birch and aspen hillsides by day, where they make their living by plucking worms from the earth. Unless they're disturbed, they fly mostly by night, and their flights are short except during the October and March migrations. Then they beat their little wings purposefully and travel thousands of miles.

Those of us who have made the woodcock's acquaintance find them elusive, mysterious, admirable, and altogether lovable. We worry about them, for their populations have been declining steadily for more than twenty years, and there is no reason to think they will recover. We still hunt them in the fall, because we know that we are the least of their problems, and because hunting them teaches us to understand and admire and love them.

And we seek them out in March, when they return from their wintering grounds, to celebrate the arrival of springtime with them.

The Song of Spring
61

I pick a cool March evening after a warm day, that delicious time of year when old snow still huddles in dirty patches under the evergreens but the fields lie bare and the earth is soft and the brooks run full with snowmelt. I hunker at the edge of a winter-flattened New England meadow, facing the pewter-and-pink western horizon, and I watch the light fade from the sky. I know it will start about the time the evening's first star winks on.

But no matter how expectant I am, the sudden buzz always startles me, both by its proximity and by its harshness. It sounds like the metallic scrape of a thumbnail across the teeth of a comb. It is, technically, a song. But it's hardly melodious. It's called, inexplicably, a "peent."

The little bird struts self-importantly on the bare ground not twenty feet from where I crouch. His chest is inflated and his long beak jabs rhythmically at the ground. He swaggers and bobs back and forth like a windup toy, buzzing like a summertime cicada. In fact, a woodcock looks like a large, boggle-eyed insect.

Abruptly he flushes. With a musical whistle of wings, he angles across the field. Then he begins to spiral upward into the pale evening sky. He rises higher and higher until he disappears from sight, although I can still hear his distant, muted twitter.

Upland Days

62

A moment later he reappears, zigzagging and parachuting back to earth like an autumn leaf on a soft breeze. As he descends, he utters a different tone, a liquid, kissing note. He lands beside me, almost precisely at the spot where I first spotted him. He must see me, for I've made no effort to hide. Yet this normally skittish wild bird ignores me, for the coy object of his passion huddles nearby. He peents, preens, struts, then flushes again, full of his heedless hot-blooded passion. He repeats his elaborate, intensely self-absorbed dance several times while the light fades from the sky and the night grows chilly.

Soon it is dark. The performance has ended. I stand, gaze up for a moment at the star-filled evening sky, then walk back out of the woods. The air still feels winter-cold. But I am warmed by the certain knowledge that my woodcock have returned once more. Spring has finally come.

Chapter 6

Woodcock Bottom

All woodcock-hunting strategies are based on the two slender facts we know about the little birds: They feed primarily on worms; and they migrate. Most strategies end here, too, because woodcock are elusive, contradictory, and unpredictable creatures—which, of course, accounts for much of their appeal.

Biologists who study woodcock for a living also find them elusive and contradictory and unpredictable. The one fact they all agree on is that woodcock are in trouble, and that loss of suitable habitat is the culprit. Otherwise, nobody knows very much about woodcock. But everybody who has made their acquaintance seems to love them.

Upland Days

64

I've flushed woodcock from the middle of newly mown hayfields, corn stubble, mature pine forests, and oak ridges. I've seen woodcock on the grass strip that divides an eight-lane highway within sight of the Boston skyline.

I once looked out the kitchen window of my suburban home and saw five woodcock under the bird feeder.

One fall I shot a woodcock that the dog had pointed under charred timbers and rusted bedsprings in a burned-out cellar hole.

On the other hand, nobody goes looking for woodcock on highway dividers or in hay fields. In fact, the best way to find woodcock is to hunt with somebody who already knows where they are. This is the only thing I know for certain about finding woodcock, although I've spent more than forty Octobers looking for them. If you know this much, however, you don't even need to know about worms and migration.

That's why several seasons ago I accepted Keith Wegener's invitation. He had a reputation. Woodcock were his passion. He called the nineteenth-century farmhouse where he lived in southwestern Maine "The Timberdoodle Inn," and his convoluted directions got me there a little after nine o'clock on a golden morning in mid-October.

Woodcock Bottom

65

We loaded our gear into his truck and turned left at the end of his driveway. A tail thumped rhythmically from the dog box in back, and Keith began to tell me about the time an old downeaster named Albert found an oak toilet seat at the town dump. It was an entertaining story, with as many twists and turns and rises and dips as the maze of dirt roads Keith took us over.

When we passed a field bordered by alders, I said, "That looks good."

"Tried it a couple times," said Keith. "Too grassy." He pronounced it "grah-ssy." "Woodcock don't like thick grass. I s'pose it's because they can't waddle around in it with their stubby little legs. Plus they can't jam their bills down through it into the ground."

A little farther on, a brook passed under the road and disappeared into some thick undergrowth. "How about there?" I said.

"Been there. Too rocky."

"Uh-uh," he said about another place that looked perfect to me. "Moss."

"Too piney," was his verdict on a sun-drenched hillside grown to a low mix of poplar and evergreen. "Acid soil. Same as moss and rocks—no worms. No worms, no woodcock."

Upland Days

66

By the time Albert had sanded down and varnished (which Keith pronounced "vanished") his new toilet seat, we had driven past at least half a dozen places that looked like the classic woodcock cover I used to find all over New England. Keith had tried them all. "Alder, popple, apple, birch whips, all worth checkin'," he said, " 'specially when they're all mingled together. But it ain't what's over their heads that woodcock mostly care about. It's what's under their feet. They like soft, loamy"—he called it "loomy"—"earth they can sink their beaks into. Mucky low places, 'specially next to a pasture so the cows can get in and tromp around and fertilize it. A nice moist hillside grown up to popple and birch saplings with a few generations of leaf mold on it is gen'rally good. Woodcock don't like it too thick and tangly on the ground. They want to be able to strut around. You want woodcock, you've got to find woodcock bottom. And the only way to find good bottom is to get offa yer own. You don't find woodcock bottom from the car window."

We drove for nearly an hour. After several punch lines, Keith had reached the point in his story where Edna, Albert's wife, had sat upon the newly installed oak toilet seat while the "vanish" was still tacky.

Woodcock Bottom

67

Abruptly he turned off the dirt road onto a barely visible pair of ruts and wedged his truck into a screen of thick brush. He got out, ambled up the road, looked back, then nodded with satisfaction. This I understood: the woodcock hunter's paranoia. A good woodcock cover is too precious to share with strangers. A car visible from the road is a certain giveaway.

By the time we had our boots laced and our shotguns uncased, Freebie, Keith's English pointer, had disappeared. Keith cocked his head, then smiled. "No bell," he said. "Let's go find her."

Freebie was locked on point less than fifty feet from the car. Keith and I moved in on either side of the dog. The woodcock flushed from under my feet. He rose, feinted, hesitated, darted, and changed direction like Michael Jordan driving the lane, and was still struggling toward the top of the alders after I had discharged both barrels. A moment later Keith's gun barked once, and the little bird tumbled down.

Freebie went to it, nudged it once with her nose, then sat down beside it—not the first good bird dog I'd met that refused to retrieve woodcock. Keith picked it up and stroked its feathers.

"Nice shot," I said.

Upland Days

68

"Woodcock ain't hard to hit, provided you give your shot pattern a chance to open up."

"I know that, dammit," I said.

"In New Zealand," he persisted, "when a big brown trout takes your dry fly, the guides tell you to sing 'God save the queen' before you set the hook. On woodcock, I try to say, 'God bless you, little timberdoodle' before I pull the trigger."

"Yeah," I muttered. "Good advice."

Keith looked around. "Where's Freebie?"

She was pointing again.

We lost track of the number of woodcock Freebie pointed in that cover. The alders had not yet dropped their leaves, so several times we only heard the whistle and twitter of wings. We missed often and gloriously. Still, we only had to hunt half the cover before we each had two birds in our game pockets.

"Whaddya think?" asked Keith. "I like to do it the way the old gentlemen hunters used to do it. Shoot a brace and call it a day."

"I like to do it that way, too," I said. "When I can manage to shoot a brace."

It took less than five minutes to drive back to The Timberdoodle Inn, barely enough time for Edna to find herself stuck to the

Woodcock Bottom

newly vanished toilet seat. As we pulled into Keith's driveway, Albert was loading her into the bed of his old Dodge pickup, toilet seat and all.

"That cover," I said to Keith, "can't be more than a mile from here."

He grinned.

"We traveled about fifty miles to get there."

"Wanted to show you some country," he said.

"And you distracted me with your endless story about Albert and Edna."

"Ayup."

I nodded. More paranoia. Keith didn't mind taking a stranger hunting, but he wanted to be sure that the stranger wouldn't be able to find the best woodcock cover in the county on his own. By the time we had finished our morning's hunt, Keith and I were no longer strangers. He trusted me enough to bring me back the short way.

We broiled our two brace of woodcock for dinner, basting them in my mother's secret sauce. Wild rice, salad greens, and broccoli spears from Keith's garden, followed by a wedge of Leigh's warm apple pie.

Upland Days

70

Some people believe woodcock are inedible. I like to promote this fallacy, on the theory that anybody who'd refuse to eat them would not try to shoot them.

Of course, it doesn't work that way. I've actually met woodcock hunters who were delighted to find somebody to give their birds to. It saved them the trouble of choking them down themselves, they claimed.

I was brought up to eat what I shot. That's how I learned what frogs' legs taste like, and it's why I quit hunting crows. So I was tempted to suggest that if those guys didn't like to eat woodcock, it would be easier—and more honorable—not to shoot them.

Still, I was happy to get their birds, because I think a broiled brace of woodcock, cooked my mother's way and served with proper ceremony and a musty red wine, is a certified delicacy.

The key to cooking lean, dark, wild meat, whether it's venison, black duck, or woodcock—or, for all I know, porcupine and raccoon—is to avoid overcooking, which makes it tough, dry, and stringy, and destroys its flavor. Blood should run to the knife when you slice into it.

Woodcock Bottom

My father was a skeptic, but since he kept bringing home woodcock, my mother experimented until she finally hit upon a sauce that sold everyone in our family.

A skinned woodcock breast is barely the size of a tennis ball. It should spend no more than ten minutes under the broiler.

Let a meal's worth (two or three breasts per person) broil for five minutes, and then baste them every minute or so with a warmed-up sauce made with one-eighth cup of water, two teaspoons of yellow mustard, one teaspoon of tomato catsup, one teaspoon of Worcestershire sauce, and two tablespoons of melted butter. This is enough sauce for six woodcock breasts.

Follow the same procedure for four mallard or black duck breasts, except double the sauce and the cooking time.

The next morning we returned, bursting with anticipation, to Keith's secret woodcock cover. We crisscrossed it for three hours. Freebie bumped one bird, which escaped unseen.

Back at the car, Keith said, "Well, they're gone. Some people believe they move on a cold front, or a north wind, or the full moon. The way I figure it, they've got a biological clock in 'em that gets 'em started, and once they start, they just keep going.

Upland Days

72

They fly by night, drop into a nice loomy place for a day or two, rest up, gobble a ration of worms, then move on. I'll keep coming here, though. There'll be more birds comin' down." He shrugged. "That's woodcock for you. They eat worms and migrate. That's about all I know."

I've hunted with Keith every October since then. Some years we find more woodcock than others, but over the long haul, according to my hunting log, the numbers have dwindled disturbingly. Lately, even on a good day, we're hard-pressed to shoot a brace apiece, and when we do, we tend to feel regretful.

We still visit that good cover he showed me on the first day we hunted together, although it doesn't look quite so good anymore. The birch and popple saplings have grown into trees, and the bottom isn't as soft and loomy as I remember it. Some days we see no chalking or drill holes or any other sign that a woodcock ever dropped into it.

Keith and I are partners now, and we'll keep roaming the back roads, looking for good woodcock bottoms and telling stories. I'm hoping that one of these Octobers I'll find out if Albert's wife ever got herself unstuck from that vanished toilet seat.

Part III

The Drummer

I know no sweeter music than the booming roar of their startled flight, and I know of nothing else which will set my heart to pounding so ecstatically. I love to hunt them. I like to bag a few of them occasionally. But better still I like to know that despite drought and flood, disease and pestilence, vermin, predators, automobiles and man, the ruffed grouse has the fortitude to survive and periodically replenish our woodlands with others of its kind.
—Burton L. Spiller
DRUMMER IN THE WOODS, 1962

Chapter 7

Birdy Places

We were bumping over a New Hampshire dirt road one golden October afternoon, Dad and Burt Spiller up front and Duke, our old setter, and I in back, when a dark shadow swooped overhead. Dad slammed on the brakes. "Did you see that?" he said.

"Great horned owl," said Burt. He peered out the car window. "I think we'd better investigate."

Dad nosed the car up a pair of old ruts that ended at a caved-in cellar hole. An old apple orchard, mingled with pine and birch and poplar, dribbled down the hillside to an alder-edged brook. "Looks real birdy," whispered Burt.

Upland Days

76

It *was* birdy. A brood of grouse exploded from the edge of the orchard, and a flight of woodcock twittered out of the birches on the hillside. When the hunt ended, Dad took out his topographic map and drew a circle on it. He labeled it "The Tattletale Owl."

"How'd you know that'd be a good cover?" I asked Burt. "You figure that owl was hunting grouse in there?"

He grinned. "No," he said. "I just noticed the apples."

Burt liked to reminisce about the wise old English setter he'd once hunted with. "That dog pointed automatically whenever he came within smelling distance of an apple tree," Burt would say, and if there was a twinkle in his eye he managed to hide it. "And by golly," he'd add, "she was right most of the time."

Burt and Dad liked to scout for new grouse covers at Burt's kitchen table. They'd hunch over a topographic map and point to the legends with the eraser end of a pencil. They looked for the dotted lines that terminated in little rectangles and the other clues to abandoned farmyards. There we might find old orchards. And where there were apples, we expected to find grouse.

Virtually all of our productive New England grouse and woodcock covers featured the apple orchards that had been planted,

Birdy Places

and ultimately abandoned, by hardy old Yankee farmers. Mankiller, Tripwire, Bullring, Henhouse, Five Aces, Crankcase—apple covers, every one.

After a few seasons of hunting with Dad and Burt, I developed a "feel" for good grouse habitat. I carried in my head a mind's-eye picture that was a composite of all those New England places we visited and revisited on autumn weekends. My mental picture remarkably resembled an Aden Lassell Ripley watercolor: a background of gold-and-crimson New Hampshire hills, a field dotted with clumps of poplar and juniper and bounded by a weathered stone wall, low edges of brush and blackberry and sprawling wild grape, a gentle gray birch hillside that sloped down to an alder-bordered brook and then rose on the other side to a thick stand of pine. Somewhere in the adjacent second-growth forest a tall lilac guarded an old cellar hole, and nearby a great flat wellstone and a cluster of toppled gravestones lay in the weeds.

Gnarled old apple trees heavy with fruit were always in the thick brushy corners and scattered over the hillside. Find apples, I knew, and you'd find grouse.

Burt, in his soft-spoken way, eventually explained to me that apples were merely the signal-beacons of likely grouse habitat.

Upland Days

"Oh, grouse do love apples," he said, "but they'll eat just about anything. If apples and grouse seem to go together, it's because the forces that created orchards were the same forces that created good grouse cover."

"I thought grouse just liked to eat apples," I said.

"Edges," Burt said. "What grouse really like are edges."

Classic grouse cover is not natural. Before farmers began to cut back the forests, ruffed grouse—and deer, turkey, bear, and, in fact, most wild creatures—were scarcer than they are now. Those farmers cut roads for their wagons, cleared pastures for their livestock, tilled fields for their crops, and, of course, planted orchards. Their clearings let in the sunlight that nourished the growth of brushy understory where grouse could find shelter from predators. Partridge berries, blueberries, wild strawberries, thornapple, clover, sumac, poplar, alder, birch—all flourished, much to the benefit of adult ruffed grouse. Insects, a staple food for chicks, abounded along the grassy field edges.

In northern New England and across the lake states, it was primarily the loggers, not the farmers, who opened the land with their tote roads and woodlots. They planted no apples, but they left roadways and islands of clear-cuts and piles of slash—offensive, perhaps, to the esthetic eye, but mighty attractive to grouse.

Birdy Places

Ruffed grouse range widely across North America. Probably the thickest populations are found in the Northeast—Pennsylvania, New York, and New England—and the lake states of Minnesota, Michigan, and Wisconsin. It's no coincidence that grouse and aspen share about the same range, whether or not apples are also present. Aspen springs up along open edges and in cleared land, and aspen buds provide vital forage for wintering grouse.

Productive cover must satisfy the bird's basic requirements of food and shelter. And everywhere, Burt Spiller's simple truth holds: Look for the edges that provide protective thickets and abundant forage; there you will find grouse.

Ruffed grouse survive because they are adaptable and smart. Studies have identified more than one hundred species of vegetation that provide food for them. They will eat almost anything available to them, depending on the season of the year: buds in winter, insects and leaves in spring and summer. In autumn, when we hunt them, grouse turn their attention to mature seeds, nuts, berries, and fruit. In good mast years, they gorge on acorns and beechnuts. They eat any kind of fruit—apples, of course, and grapes, another favorite. One of my best New Hampshire grouse covers surrounds an ancient pear orchard.

Upland Days

80

Because many predators besides men with guns and dogs hunt them, grouse never stray far from the protective shelter of a stand of evergreens. A good food source without an escape route to nearby sanctuary, or vice versa, rarely harbors many grouse.

The key characteristic of those classic mind's-eye pictures of mine is not really apple. It's variety. Those Ripley watercolors feature topography breaks: the hillsides, ridge points, and stream bottoms that make grouse hunting a test of strength and stamina for both man and dog. Vegetation transition zones dominate those pictures. Grouse live where alder and aspen merge into pine, where apple mixes with juniper, where briar borders birch.

Grouse, like people, follow daily routines. They are not early risers. They roost in evergreen thickets, and stay in the trees until the sun melts the frost from the goldenrod. By mid-morning they are basking on sun-drenched knolls or pecking gravel and dusting their feathers along the edges of dirt roads. They feed most heavily in the afternoon, and when the shadows begin to lengthen they work their way back to their roosts. Good cover allows grouse to do all of these things without moving far, for they are notorious stay-at-homes.

Once adult grouse establish their territory, they rarely stray far from it. They raise their broods there and share it with as many

Birdy Places

of their relatives as the area can sustain. That's why a good grouse cover will hold birds for as long as it continues to provide food and shelter. Burt Spiller's old string of covers in southern Maine and New Hampshire remained productive for the ten years that I hunted with him, and for many years afterward.

Gradually, though, forests reclaimed the old pastures and fields. Mankiller and Tripwire, Bullring and Crankcase—they no longer felt birdy. The edges disappeared, and so did the grouse.

In 1972, in his Introduction to the Crown reprint of Burton L. Spiller's classic *Grouse Feathers*, my father wrote: "Looking back over the years I've hunted grouse, nearly four decades now, it seems to me that each high point in the cycle has not been quite so high as the previous one—and each low point has been a little lower. That isn't to say that the grouse *couldn't* come back, given the chance. No species of wildlife is hardier, none better able to survive heavy shooting, predation, or the bitter winds of winter. But I do know they will never return to our Old Schoolhouse Cover, because a power line cuts through it now, or to many other 'birdy' places of yesteryear where the old apple orchards and wild grape tangles have been bulldozed away to make room for more houses and more sterile ribbons of macadam."

Upland Days

82

Gordon Gullion, a wildlife biologist who devoted a long and distinguished career to the study of ruffed grouse, chastised Dad for his fatalism. On December 24, 1972, just a few months after *Grouse Feathers* hit the bookstores, Gullion wrote Dad a letter:

"Spiller apparently hunted his grouse in the years when the forests were still quite young, just regenerating from earlier devastation by logging and fire. For grouse are dependent upon young forests—and a forest more than about twenty years old will soon lose its ability to provide these birds with the cover they need.

"If 'partridge' hunting passes out of the picture in New England, it'll be the fault of those who are most interested in this sport—for failing to become active in the political arena and supporting the types of programs that it takes to maintain the young popple forests which these grouse require.

"If you continue to let your Eastern forests grow old and be preserved from ecological rejuvenation, then you'd better put up your shooting pieces and spend pleasant fall afternoons recalling the good old days—while we're busy

Birdy Places

shooting grouse out here [in Minnesota] in our young forests.

"If you let forest preservation and selective cutting continue to be the primary management tool in your wildlife areas, you'll lose not only your grouse, but your woodcock, deer, bear, beaver, and snowshoe hares as well. But if you'll get on the backs of the foresters and insist that they do something positive for wildlife—find or develop a market for your popple stands (scarce as they are in many areas) and then start clear-cutting those stands in patches no larger than 10-acres in extent, you'll be amazed at how fast grouse and other wildlife will repopulate some of your now barren habitats. How'd you like to have 12 grouse out from underfoot in twenty minutes—like I had on a couple of occasions toward the end of our season this year?"

I, for one, would like it very much. My old dependable grouse and woodcock covers—Tripwire, Hippie House, Stick Farm, Five Aces—are no longer dependable. I've been chasing pointing dogs through the woods every fall for more than forty years, and my hunting logs tell the tale: We aren't finding as many birds as we used to.

Upland Days

84

Scientific surveys throughout the Northeast and Upper Midwest reflect my hunting experience: Ruffed grouse and woodcock populations have been declining steadily and acutely for a long time.

It's tempting to blame urban sprawl, highway construction, acid rain, pesticides, predation, hunting pressure, natural cycles, or bad luck.

"Mainly, it's loss of suitable habitat," says Dan Dessecker, the forest wildlife biologist for the Ruffed Grouse Society (RGS). "We've actually got as much woodland in the Northeast now as we had a hundred years ago. Back then, the farmers kept the land open. Now it's reverted to mature forest, which makes terrible grouse and woodcock habitat. In fact, the whole forest community—including hundreds of species of songbirds—is suffering from loss of habitat."

The late Greg Sepik, who devoted his life to studying woodcock, seconded Dessecker's assessment. "Woodcock and grouse need a thick mixed understory—grasses, briars, shrubs, vines, young alders, and aspen and birch. Mature trees block sunlight from the ground. No sun, no understory. No understory, no cover and food. No cover and food, no birds."

Birdy Places

As Dessecker says, "Although there are exceptions, a typical ruffed grouse or woodcock cover provides quality habitat for only about as long as the life of a good bird dog. Stragglers persist, but birds are found in abundance for only a decade or so, just as long as it takes for the individual trees to sort out which ones will grow and survive and which will wither and die in the shade cast by their taller neighbors. As these young, dense forests grow and become more open, the ruffed grouse, woodcock, golden-winged warbler, yellow-breasted chat, and a host of other critters are forced to go elsewhere. So, too, are those of us who venture afield each fall after grouse and woodcock."

The solution? "Clear-cutting," says Dessecker. "What we call 'clear-cut regeneration.' Open up the forest, let in the sunshine, and the birds will prosper. It's like surgery. Done carelessly, it can kill you. But done scientifically, clear-cutting brings health and diversity back to a forest."

The RGS gives money and expertise to more than four hundred public land habitat improvement projects in twenty-five states and five Canadian provinces. These Management Area Projects (MAP) employ clear-cuts of anywhere from five to one hundred acres, which are rotated over the years, so that a MAP

Upland Days

always provides diverse habitat. RGS biologists confirm that bird populations on these projects have prospered.

The Coverts Project, which works with RGS and the Extension Service in eleven Northeastern states, advises private landowners how to manage their woodlots for wildlife. "Our message," says Steve Broderick, extension forester at the University of Connecticut, "is simple: If you leave a forest alone, you are *not* doing the best thing for wildlife."

In spite of its proven effectiveness, habitat regeneration by clear-cutting is still a tough sell. "People love big old trees," says Dessecker. "They'd rather 'protect' game birds by reducing bag limits and shortening seasons. It's frustrating, because all the evidence proves that it's a habitat—not a harvest—issue."

So how does he answer those who oppose clear-cutting? "I tell them that baby trees need love, too," he concludes.

Burt Spiller has been gone for more than twenty-five years. But if we continue to open up the land, creating the edges and variety that Burt always looked for, there is still hope that ruffed grouse, like his stories, will not only live on, but thrive.

Chapter 8

How to Miss Flying Grouse

The grouse flushed just as I stepped into the field. Instead of squirting through the hemlocks or twisting back through the alders or diving over the hill, this bird chose to do exactly what you'd expect a grouse to do—the unexpected.

He flew across the open field right in front of me.

He looked as big as a turkey as he lumbered through the air: an easy, slow-motion, right-to-left crossing shot. I mounted my gun, swung smoothly, and squeezed the trigger. When he didn't tumble, I kept swinging and pulled the second trigger.

The grouse flipped his tail at me and continued across the field. The last I saw of him, he was scaling over the trees toward a distant swamp.

Upland Days

88

A minute later Keith joined me in the field. "Git 'im?" he asked.

"Nope."

"What happened?"

I looked him in the eye. "That bird was just flying too damn slow."

Keith nodded admiringly. "That's a new one."

"Thank you," I said.

Sporting magazines regularly publish articles titled, with minor variations, "How to Shoot Grouse." They are sober, practical treatises, often accompanied by charts that factor such variables as wing speed, shot pattern, and angle of ascent, along with optimistic diagrams depicting birds and shot patterns colliding in midair.

These articles take gleeful delight in pointing out that while grouse don't fly as fast as sea ducks or doves or many other shotgun targets, they rarely fly straight or at constant speeds, and they are uncanny in their ability to put trees and brush between themselves and a man with a shotgun. Like crafty old major-league pitchers, grouse love to throw change-ups and curveballs, sinkers and knuckleballs. They dart and dip and move at unpredictable angles. Then, just often enough to keep you off balance,

How to Miss Grouse

they give you a high hard one. They usually flush from unexpected places at unexpected times. Then there are factors such as sun, which is always in your eyes, hilly and brushy terrain, uncertain footing, wind, and—well, if it isn't one thing, it's another.

Readiness and sharp reflexes help. You have to be mighty quick and alert to mount your gun, take aim, and snap off a shot in one second. During that time a ruffed grouse can fly nearly sixty feet. Even a woodcock moving at a leisurely 25 mph—under a head of steam, woodcock can fly quite a bit faster—travels thirty-seven feet in that single second.

Sober and informative magazine essays generally advise aspiring upland marksmen to put in time at the sporting-clays range, spend fortunes on customized shotguns, practice dry-mounting and swinging in the privacy of their own living rooms, study the habits of *Bonasa umbellus*, invest in thoroughbred pointers or setters, and then spend another fortune on professional dog training.

It makes pretty entertaining reading. But it occurs to me that these articles might dupe naive readers into believing that shooting a flying grouse is actually a skill, implying that it can be learned and improved.

Upland Days

Anyone who's hunted with shotguns for a while knows that this is arrant nonsense. I've been tromping the uplands for nearly half a century now. I've hunted with skeet hotshots, grizzled outdoor writers, old-time market hunters, as well as rank beginners. I've kept a detailed journal of my days afield, and I can assure you that the only useful wisdom on the subject of hitting flying grouse with a shotgun derives directly from the Eternal and Immutable Law of Averages.

Wingshooting skill, crafty woodsmanship, and talented pointing dogs have nothing to do with it.

Here are the hard facts: For every twelve grouse flushed, four escape unseen; of the eight that the hunter glimpses, four are out of range or otherwise do not get shot at; of the four shots that the hunter take, three are misses.

Put it another way: For every twelve grouse my partners and I have encountered in fifty years of hunting, we've shot exactly one. I've seen the hunting logs of many other upland gunners, including some who write how-to-shoot-grouse articles, and their records are virtually identical to mine.

With all due respect for those writers and other experts who recommend shooting quick or shooting slow, snap shooting or leading and following through, understanding angles and flight

How to Miss Grouse

speed and wind direction or consulting hypnotists and psychics, practicing and calculating or relying on instinct, using bigger or smaller shot sizes, lighter or heavier shotguns, doubles or autoloaders, big or small bores, tight or open chokes . . . the truth is: IT DOESN'T MATTER.

Over the long haul, you'll shoot one out of twelve—and there's nothing you can do to change it.

All these how-to-shoot-grouse articles, therefore, serve no purpose except to cruelly raise the expectations of unwary readers. This guarantees disappointment. No matter what combination of skill, luck, perseverance, woodsmanship, and experience he carries afield with him, every grouse hunter will fail to score eleven out of twelve times. No magazine article can ever change that.

The Law of Averages will take care of that one-in-twelve triumph. What grouse hunters *really* need is a repertoire of explanations, excuses, and alibis for those eleven failures.

Here's where my half century of missing flying grouse can help. So, as a service to the inexperienced hunter, I have scoured my journals and consulted my partners and other experts and have compiled a compendium of excuses which, I am confident, any beginning grouse hunter can adapt to his needs.

Upland Days

92

Nothing beats sharp reflexes, a nimble imagination, and decades of practice. The master of the alibi can snap off a quick excuse in a wingbeat, and some gunners seem to be blessed with a God-given talent for it. "That bird was flying too damn slow," for example, I humbly offer as a classic.

Novices shouldn't expect to come up with anything as original and inspired as that one right away. Begin with modest expectations. Don't be ashamed to plagiarize. Remember: Most of the good excuses have already been used. But they have survived the test of time. They still do the job. Even experienced alibiers fall into predictable patterns. You can learn from the experts.

The rules of effective alibi-making are few and simple:

1. Understand that there *is* an explanation for every miss. Your job is to come up with it without hesitating or bumbling. "I thought I was right on him," or, "Dunno what happened that time," are *not* excuses.
2. Never blame your own lack of skill. "I didn't lead him enough," or "I lifted my head just as I shot," mark you as an amateur of the alibi. Instead, deflect the fault to your

How to Miss Grouse

equipment. "I had him centered. This old gun never did pattern number eights well." Or, "The old blunderbuss just hasn't hung right since I lost all that weight." In a pinch, haul out the oldest and most shopworn excuse of all: "My safety stuck again." It still works.

3. Emphasize the difficulty of the shot you missed. "He was out of range. Never should've pulled the trigger." Or "Just caught a glimpse of him as he darted around that tree. It would've been a miraculous shot."

4. Never give the bird any credit. That's just a backward way of blaming yourself. "He caught me off guard," or, "He kept that big pine tree between us," simply makes you appear inept. Instead, shift the blame to the elements: "That big pine jumped right in front of me, took the whole load. I was right on that bird, too. Come here. Take a look at this tree." Or "The sun popped out from behind the clouds just as I squeezed off my shot. Blinded me for a second." Or "I swung right up against a poplar sapling." Or "I was horse-collared by a grapevine. Did damn well just to get a shot off." Your gunning partner (who, remember, wants you to accept *his* excuses with a straight face) will nod and murmur sympathetically.

Upland Days

5. Whenever possible, deflect blame on to your partner. Be cautious—you must be subtle and phrase these alibis carefully lest you provoke a did-not/did-too discussion that will convert all future excuses into debates. Try these: "I could've taken him easy, but he was headed your way. I pulled off at the last second so you could take him. What happened?" Or, "You kinda got out in front a little, didn't you? If we'd done it right, we'd've had that bird cornered." The advantage of this tactic, of course, is that it immediately challenges your partner to come up with a better excuse than you did, and you have preempted the entire blame-your-partner category of alibis. When you accept his excuse—as you must—you've assured yourself of an understanding audience for all the rest of yours, however weak they may be.

6. Blame the dog. If it's your own dog, it's easy. After you miss, simply yell, "Burt! Dammit! What do you think you're *doing?*" To guarantee sympathy and understanding, mumble something about Burt's ancestors, that charlatan trainer in Vermont, your wife (who insists that Burt sleep in the bedroom), or your kids (who throw objects for Burt but fail to use the command "fetch"). If it's your partner's

How to Miss Grouse

dog, it's trickier but still possible. Never blame his dog directly. Instead, shift the burden of alibi-making to your partner. "Was Mack over there with you when that bird got up?" Or "It looked like Mack was making game, and the next thing I knew . . ."

7. That one-in-twelve occasion when your shot brings a puff of feathers and a dead bird, if you handle it deftly, sets you up for the rest of the season. Never credit either your skill or your luck. Instead, use your moment of triumph to establish the excuses you know you'll be needing. "Thought I was right on him, but the sun was in my eyes. I shot at the blur." Or "My safety kept jamming. Got that shot off in the nick of time." Or "I think Freebie bumped him. That bird was nearly out of range when I shot."

In the beginning, it's advisable to hunt alone. Practice your alibi-making on an imaginary partner. At first you'll fumble around, and your excuses will sound pretty lame. But if you work at it, you'll find that acceptable alibis begin to tumble swiftly and gracefully from your lips.

When you start believing them yourself, you're ready to hunt with a partner.

Upland Days

96

If you spend enough time in the woods, eventually a grouse will give you an unbelievably easy shot, say, a slow right-to-left across an open field. You will, of course, miss it. Nothing in your well-practiced repertoire of alibis has prepared you for this. You'll be tempted to shrug and blurt, "How could I have missed? Never had a better chance in my life."

Don't do it. Instead, recognize that this is the moment of truth, the ultimate challenge, the occasion that years of alibi practice have pointed to.

Now is the time to convert disaster into triumph. Look your partner in the eye, shake your head, and tell him, "That bird was just flying too damn slow."

He will be awed. And isn't that what grouse hunting is all about?

Chapter 9

The Chipmunk Hypothesis

After several lean grouse seasons in a row, I was feeling darkly pessimistic on this particular Opening Day. But as we drove through the crimson-and-gold New England countryside, Keith was whistling and drumming his fingers on the steering wheel.

"What're you so damn chipper about?" I finally asked.

"Opening Day, my boy," he said. "A brand-new season. What could be finer?"

"The prospect of scaring up a few birds would help," I said.

"Oh, it's gonna be good. Big partridge year. Mark my words."

"What makes you think so?"

He turned and grinned at me. "Chipmunks," he said.

"Huh?"

He shrugged. "I've been seeing lots of chipmunks this summer. Chipmunks mean grouse. Q.E.D."

I snorted. "How do you figure that?"

"Grouse and chipmunks. They operate on the same cycle. Lots of chipmunks mean lots of grouse. See?"

"Actually, no."

"Acorns, son."

"Oh, sure," I grumbled. "Acorns. Makes sense to me."

I wanted to believe him. I wanted to share his enthusiasm. I'd hunted through several grouse cycles. Each low point convinced me that this time it was permanent, that there were so few birds they would never recover. And each time, gradually, they had come back. Grouse are remarkably resilient and adaptive birds.

But chipmunks?

Fifteen minutes later, Keith pulled up to the gas pumps in front of a ramshackle Mom 'n' Pop store where two dirt roads intersected. A young guy wearing overalls and a black beard ambled out. He planted his forearms on the roof of our wagon, bent down, and peered inside. He saw two men wearing leather-faced pants sitting up front, one Brittany and one English pointer whining in back, and, on the floor, two 20-gauge doubles, several

The Chipmunk Hypothesis

boxes of shotgun shells, leather boots, shooting vests, check cords, belled collars, and a wicker picnic basket.

He scratched his beard for a moment, processing the clues, and then grinned. "Bird hunting, eh? Well, lissen. You boys wanna know where you can find yerselves some pa'tridges?"

"Partridges?" said Keith. "The hell with partridges. We're looking for chipmunks."

Whenever a long day of chasing pointing dogs through Mankiller and Hippie House and Stick Farm and our other grouse covers leaves our gun barrels clean, Keith and I don't blame our bird-finding skills or our luck or our dogs. Instead, we comfort ourselves with this handy explanation: The cycle must be down this year.

And when the other members of our New England grouse-shooting network also report slim pickins, even taking into account the Machiavellian secrecy of partridge fanatics (we do not necessarily trust each other), we deduce a trend.

If the reports are consistently grim throughout the season, we assume we know why. Grouse populations are cyclical. Always have been, always will be. Some years are better than others, and there's nothing you can do about it except wait it out. As Keith philosophizes, "That's how she goes."

Oh, I know that tromping through the same string of covers behind mediocre bird dogs for six autumn weekends a year is not the most scientific method for sampling the grouse population. But I keep careful count of the birds I flush, I do not count second starts, and I do it year after year. So do my friends. I find patterns. And the patterns I find generally seem to match those observed by others who hunt grouse in New England—and even in other regions.

According to my hunting journal, grouse populations in New England rise and fall on a crude ten-year cycle.

According to Keith, so do chipmunks.

Those who are seriously concerned about the health of grouse populations focus not on cycles, which are natural, and therefore acceptable, short-term phenomena, and which, by definition, include an upturn for every downturn. Nowadays, we worry about the long-term picture. Each downturn of the cycle seems to dip lower, while the ensuing upturn doesn't bounce back quite as high. Biologists blame it on habitat loss—suburban and industrial sprawl, and the expansion of the highway system, certainly,

The Chipmunk Hypothesis

but especially the loss of the thick understory that makes prime grouse cover. And this, of course, is occurring as second-growth forests all over the northern tier of states mature.

Habitat loss is measurable and understandable. It can also, at least in theory, be reversed. The Ruffed Grouse Society promotes selective clear-cutting as the most promising way of addressing this unhappy trend and restoring healthy grouse numbers.

But regardless of the long-term scarcity or abundance of grouse, cycles will continue, and they'll continue to be mysterious.

I read somewhere that ruffed grouse abundance in New England fluctuates on the same four-year cycle as Atlantic salmon, UFO sightings, German pork prices, plankton yields in Lake Michigan, and cheese consumption. The article offered the cautious thesis that some of these correspondences might not actually be coincidental.

Nowhere else have I heard of a four-year grouse cycle. But I am intrigued by the idea that the same forces that push up pork prices and cause people to see UFOs actually influence the reproduction and survival rates of grouse.

Even more interesting is the possibility that eating cheese causes grouse to multiply.

Upland Days

I've never met a serious grouse hunter who didn't notice and wonder and worry and speculate about his beloved bird's erratic and dramatic population booms and busts. Duck and deer hunters might observe that the abundance of their chosen quarry might seem to be declining or increasing over a ten- or twenty-year period. But for grouse hunters, it's a puzzling, endlessly fascinating, year-to-year phenomenon.

Perhaps if duck hunters were more observant and kept the kind of careful records that grouse hunters tend to keep, they'd notice comparable "cycles" in duck populations. In other words, maybe grouse population cycles are no different from the fluctuations in the numbers of other wild creatures. Maybe the real difference lies in the kinds of people who love to hunt ruffed grouse. Whatever. The fact remains: Grouse hunters are constitutionally unable to engage in significant conversations with each other without sharing and debating their theories on population cycles.

Of course, if there were a scientifically valid explanation, there would be no need for speculation, and much of what fascinates us about this mysterious bird would be taken from us.

John Alden Knight, the creator of the solunar theory, noted that the population ups and downs of ruffed grouse correlated with the cycles of solar radiation. Burt Spiller often cited the pe-

The Chipmunk Hypothesis

riodic appearance of snowy owls as a sure-fire predictor of a sharp decline in grouse numbers. Dan Holland, with whom I hunted a few times, observed that grouse numbers seemed to fluctuate the same as those of rabbits, except that grouse populations crashed a year or two after rabbits.

For all I know, Keith is right. Maybe chipmunks and acorns and grouse numbers are synchronous.

Still, correlation is not the same thing as causation.

These cycles are not simply the rationalizations of unskilled or unlucky hunters. The periodic ups and downs of grouse populations have been observed and studied for centuries. In 1721, grouse numbers had declined so dramatically in Quebec that the provincial governor outlawed shooting. An abrupt disappearance of birds was observed in New Hampshire in 1831. New York market hunters experienced a sharp downturn in grouse numbers after the Civil War; and ever since that time, biologists and others have observed, studied, and speculated on the phenomenon. Their research proves that grouse populations do fluctuate cyclically—and regularly and predictably.

In his book *Ruffed Grouse,* published in 1947, Knight speculated at length on the phenomenon of grouse population cycles. He noted that they occurred independent of region, quality of habitat, or weather. Cyclical crashes were seen in both England and America in 1933, and in New England and the Midwest in 1944. Knight's research showed that the cycles made one complete revolution every eight to fourteen years—eleven years, on an average—although within each cycle there were fluctuations and cycles within cycles.

Gordon Gullion, who devoted his life to the study of grouse and grouse habitat, put the cycle at ten years, and found, furthermore, that the population crashes came predictably on years ending in 2 or 3—1933, 1943, 1952, 1963, 1973, 1982. Gullion conducted his studies primarily in Minnesota, but the latter three of those years provided me with some pretty grim grouse hunting in New England, too.

The graph of a grouse population cycle does not look like the classic bell-shaped curve. Rather, it describes a long ascending slope followed by an abrupt descent. Grouse numbers increase gradually over the ten- or eleven-year period, rising and falling erratically here and there, until they reach their peak. Then, in the short space of a season or two, they crash and start over.

But why?

Theories abound. Keith's chipmunk hypothesis holds that grouse flourish in years when the oaks produce a heavy acorn

The Chipmunk Hypothesis

crop (which, of course, nourishes both grouse and chipmunks). But as he explains it, it's not simply that grouse like to eat acorns. Abundant acorns, in other words, do not cause grouse to flourish. Rather, it's that oak and grouse—and chipmunk—cycles coincide. Good mast years are good grouse years, but there are other, mysterious variables at work.

Those of us who love ruffed grouse pay special attention to springtime weather. A wet, cold, nesting season takes a harsh toll on newly hatched chicks. Perhaps such weather conditions occur cyclically, although the research hasn't proven it.

Diseases and parasites can create epidemics. Predators, of which grouse have many, can wipe out young broods. Hawks and foxes might ignore grouse and be content to hunt cottontails as long as they are abundant. But when they've decimated the rabbit population, they have to turn to more challenging prey like grouse. That, at least, was how Dan Holland explained why grouse numbers tend to plummet a few years after cottontail numbers do.

Several turn-of-the-century studies attempted to isolate the key variable. They postulated, among other things, poaching, market hunting, forest fires, severe winters, wet springs, dry summers, ticks, foxes, goshawks, dispersal, and migration. A report from New York State, attempting to account for the crash of grouse numbers in 1906–07, speculated that "the best bet [was] an unhappy combination of the cold wet spring, the unusual abundance of predators, and an epidemic of some disease or parasite." The unlucky coincidence of several negative factors, in other words.

It's doubtful that a single variable can be pinpointed as the cause of grouse cycles. Nothing in nature works in isolation. Ruffed grouse are part of an infinitely complex web of relationships. Weather, predation, disease, food, habitat—and, yes, for all we know, sunspots, chipmunks, and cheese consumption—are all woven together. Each factor affects all the others. Tug on one thread and the whole pattern changes.

If prime habitat promotes high grouse numbers, then a heavy population of grouse will attract predators, parasites, and germs. As these scourges feed off grouse, their numbers will grow. And when they have decimated the grouse, they, in turn, will experience a sharp downturn in their populations. This leaves the surviving grouse free to start rebuilding their numbers.

It's nature's way of maintaining the vigor of the species. In times of disease, predation, or severe weather, the weak die while the fittest survive to pass their good genes along to future gener-

The Chipmunk Hypothesis

ations. This is Darwin 101, and it works for grouse, owls, germs, and chipmunks.

It also works for trees. Gullion discovered that during the upswings of the Midwestern grouse cycle, winter birds fed heavily on the male flower buds of aspens. These buds, Gullion surmised, provided especially nutritious and efficient forage for grouse, giving them the strength and health to evade predators, to survive harsh winters, and to procreate bountifully in the spring.

Gullion also concluded that when grouse turn from aspen to other less nourishing food sources such as hazel, birch, and ironwood, they have to spend more time and expend more energy in feeding. This, he speculated, makes them more vulnerable to predators, parasites, disease, and the vagaries of weather. Fewer birds survive the winter to reproduce in the spring, and newborn chicks are weaker.

But why do these birds stop eating aspen buds? Gullion made an interesting discovery, which he suggested might explain the connection between what grouse eat and the fluctuations in their numbers. Trees have survival mechanisms, too. When aspens are stressed by overbrowsing, which occurs when grouse are abundant, they produce a chemical that grouse (and other creatures) cannot digest efficiently. But when grouse numbers decrease, the aspens are no longer stressed, so they stop producing their defensive chemical. And again, in the cycle of things, grouse resume feeding on them.

And so it goes. Cycles within cycles. It's nature's way. Hunters can resent it or admire it, and we can help grouse by supporting habitat improvement projects and research. But cycles will continue, and nothing will change that. All we can do is keep an eye out for chipmunks.

Field Journal

Burton L. Spiller and Grampa Grouse, circa 1948.

Burt Spiller and the author's father, H. G. "Tap" Tapply, circa 1952 (*above*).

The author, very young, with his single-shot 20-gauge Savage, his first woodcock, and Duke, who pointed it (*right*).

Burt Spiller (*left*) wrote *Fishin' Around* as well as classic grouse-hunting books.

Duke, the raw-boned setter (*below*).

Duke, holding a rare point on a woodcock.

Partridge Shortenin', by G. Grouse. The title page.

100 copies of
Partridge Shortenin'
were privately published in 1949.

To Grampa Grouse—
the Bird Hunter (on his birthday
October 9, 1944), by H. G. Tapply

Grampa, with grouse in his jeans.

"Tap," one of the masters.

One of those glorious upland days in New England.

Burt always said: "Find apples and you'll find grouse" (*above*).

Reloading with fumbling fingers after missing with both barrels (*right*).

A rare blessing from the Red Gods of grouse hunting (*below*).

Early-season foliage makes for hard shooting . . . but easy looking.

The old Yankee farmers cleared the land and left prime grouse cover—and their stones—behind (*above*).

Keith Wegener, Freebie, and a Maine woodcock (*right*).

Keith and Freebie take a break to talk hunting strategies.

On the old road into the Hippie House cover.

Burt and the author, taking a brea

Chapter 10

Grudge Grouse

"The only thing I know for sure about partridge," Doc used to say, "is that they will always do the unexpected, bless 'em."

By the time I started hunting ruffed grouse with him, Doc had been tromping the New England uplands for about thirty years. I respected his wisdom, even if I didn't quite understand it.

"Take the hot corner in Five Aces," Doc would explain. "Now any self-respecting partridge who's pecking apples under that old lightning-struck Baldwin will hear the dog's bell and us thrashing through the woods, so he'll scurry under that thick juniper where the two stone walls meet, and he'll hunker there 'til he's sure we're on his track. Then, just about the time we're pushing through the alders at one end, he'll flush out of range from the other end, making sure he's got that screen of hemlocks between him and us as he glides down the hill toward the swamp. Now that's smart."

When I'd start to speak, Doc would hold up his hand. "You're thinking that if *we're* smart, one of us circles around ahead of him to cut him off. That *is* smart. But not smart enough. Because that's when our grouse holds there in the cover and waits for us to walk past him. Then he flushes out from behind us." Doc would shrug. "Course, you can't plan on him doing that, either. That's the time he'll decide to fly right at your face. Or he might give you an easy going-away shot—except just when you've got him mounted like a lollipop over your front sight and are touching your trigger, he'll take a quick left turn. Or right. Unless you expect it. Then he'll keep going straightaway."

"So," I said, "there's no sense in trying to outwit them. Is that it?"

"Hell, no. Trying to outwit them is the point of it."

Doc always tipped his cap to the grouse that fooled him. He knew that he had never shot a stupid grouse, nor had he ever truly outsmarted one. He credited the Red Gods or the Law of Averages or the intersection of orbiting planets and stars whenever a grouse fell to his old Winchester 20-gauge double.

When he picked up a bird he'd shot, he clucked and cooed and smoothed its feathers. "Lucky shot," he always said, and although Doc was a crack wingshot, I knew he meant it.

Grudge Grouse

111

A smart grouse knew how to put the only pine tree in the cover between himself and the man with the shotgun. A smart grouse zigged when you expected him to zag, held tight when you expected him to run, flapped slowly across an open field when you knew that was the one escape route he would never take. Being outsmarted by a grouse never bothered Doc. In fact, it seemed to delight him.

But occasionally he encountered birds that flaunted his superior intelligence. Such grouse, Doc believed, should have been content to fool him. Instead, they chose to make a fool of him.

Doc believed there were rules of fair play that applied equally to grouse and grouse hunters, and the fact that he couldn't clearly articulate those rules did not convince him that they weren't self-evident. Doc never shot a grouse off the ground or a stone wall or out of a tree. He expected comparable consideration from the bird.

Any grouse that violated the rules of the game received the ultimate malediction: Doc "grudged" him.

Doc did not bestow grudgehood lightly. In all the years we hunted together, he only grudged a handful of grouse. A bird that flushed as we stepped out of the car, while our shotguns were still cased, was likely to get grudged. Doc would grudge any grouse that flapped up into a tree and sat there staring at him, re-

Upland Days

fusing to fly until the moment Doc stooped to pick up a stick to throw at it.

Twice I remember Doc grudging grouse that waited until he'd broken open his shotgun, laid it on the ground, and unzipped his trousers before deciding it was safe to glide across an open field.

When Doc grudged a bird, it became personal.

Doc shot scores of ruffed grouse during the middle decades of this century. He readily admits to having missed hundreds, and he continues to insist that every bird he downed was a lucky shot.

Doc hung up his old Winchester a quarter of a century ago, and now, when he reminisces about those days when grouse were abundant in our New England covers, he mostly remembers the grudge birds. He speaks of them with a mixture of admiration and embarrassment and contempt.

"Remember," he said to me recently, "that sneaky S.O.B. in Tripwire?"

I nodded. It was a crisp October morning about thirty years ago. We had hunted the first half of one of our favorite New Hampshire covers, and Doc had whistled in Duke, his big-going setter, unloaded his shotgun, sat on the ground, and pulled out his

Grudge Grouse

pipe and tobacco pouch. I unloaded and sat beside him. We had moved two birds from the hidden orchard and missed them both. Now we sat by the hemlock-rimmed swamp, and while Doc fired up his pipe and I munched an apple, we debated whether we should pursue those two grouse or continue along our usual route.

We'd been sitting there for about five minutes before the grouse chose to fly. He flapped out of a hemlock not twenty feet from us, lumbered across the open orchard—a ridiculously easy shot for a man with a loaded gun—gave a derisive flip of his tail-feathers, and dipped into the swamp.

Doc sat there with his empty gun across his lap and glared into the distance. Then he cupped his hand around his mouth and yelled: "I *grudge* thee!"

He turned to me. "That bird behaved dishonorably. He purposely humiliated me. He has earned grudgehood. I hereby declare him my Nemesis, and I shall hunt him down and slay him honorably. And you," he added, jabbing his finger at my chest, "will leave him to me."

Doc mumbled about his grudge bird for the rest of the day. "Did you see him?" he said. "He had beady eyes. He sneered at me. I heard him chuckling. Oh, he knew exactly what he was doing, that one."

Upland Days

114

The next weekend when we stepped into Tripwire, Doc turned to me. "Remember," he said, "that's *my* grudge bird."

Doc took the route that would lead him to the edge of the hemlock swamp where his grudge bird lived, while I took the left flank. As we approached the battleground, I heard Doc say, "Duke's making game.... Easy, boy.... Okay. A point. Now I got you, Nemesis."

Two shots came a moment later. "Well?" I called.

"Got 'em both," Doc said conversationally. "Pair of woodcock. Atta boy, Duke. Good—"

And at that moment I heard the roar of grouse wings from Doc's direction. "*Blast* you!" he yelled. "I double-grudge you!"

When I arrived at his side, he was standing there staring into the distance. "Duke was just bringing me that second woodcock," he muttered, "and I was on one knee with my empty gun on the ground—again—holding out my hand and telling Duke what a good dog he was, and that's when the devil decided to flush."

The next time we hunted Tripwire, Doc left Duke in the car. "Guerrilla tactics," he said. "Time for a little stealth and cunning of our own. I'll sneak up on the knave. Beat him at his own crafty game."

Grudge Grouse

I slipped through the orchard while Doc crept along the hemlock edge, and when we arrived at his grudge bird's lair, I heard him mutter, "Gotcha now, Old Scratch. Surprised, eh? My gun is loaded, and you are doomed. Now . . . fly!"

There came a pause. Then Doc's voice rose. "Fly, I said. . . . Did you hear me? I said *fly*!"

A moment later I heard him yell, "Wait, gol dang you! Come back here."

Afterward he told me what had happened. "He was sitting there on the stone wall, craning his neck and smirking at me with those beady eyes of his. I told him to fly. I *commanded* him to fly. Instead, he hopped off the wall and slinked away. He never flew. He just . . . walked away."

As October slipped into November, we tried all of our normally reliable stratagems and variations on each in an effort to make Doc's grudge bird play fair. We hunted the cover backward. We hit it first thing in the morning, and we waited until the afternoon shadows were growing long. We hunted it twice in the same day. We hunted it with the dog and without the dog. Doc and I swapped routes.

Nothing worked. Doc's grudge bird was always there, and he always managed to squeeze through a hole in our formation.

Upland Days

Twice he gave me easy passing shots, but I never pulled the trigger. I had my orders. Doc would never have forgiven me if I'd fired at his grudge grouse.

Doc never got a shot at him.

The last Saturday of November that year was one of those gloomy days when the air numbs your fingers and little pellets of hard snow spit down from a low gray sky and bite your face, when birds are scarce and wild and your mind wanders to a Thermos of hot coffee and the comfort of the car's heater. We saved Tripwire for our last hunt of the last day of the season.

By then Doc's grudge had hardened into an obsession. "Today," he vowed as we climbed out of the car, "he dies. This entire season—nay, my entire lifetime of grouse hunting—has pointed to this day and this place. Today, all wrongs will be righted. Today, justice will be done."

He glanced at me, and perhaps he read something on my face, because he nodded and said, "You'll see, boy. You'll see."

We moved quietly down the now-leafless alder and poplar slope, working our way to the hidden orchard, and with no foliage between us, I could watch Doc. He kept Duke at heel, and he carried his Winchester at port arms. His jaw was thrust forward, and I could hear him mumbling.

Grudge Grouse

117

He crept along the edge of the hemlocks where his grudge bird lived, and as I watched, he paused, slid a couple steps to his left, pivoted, and raised his shotgun to his shoulder.

The roar of the flushing grouse came almost simultaneously with the report of Doc's shotgun. It echoed through the empty woods.

He broke open his gun, and I saw him grin. "Hah!" he said. "Gotcha. That'll teach you." He stood there for a moment, and then he disappeared into the hemlocks.

I arrived there as he emerged from the thicket. I saw the bulge in his game pocket. "What happened?" I asked.

Doc knelt on the ground. "When you grudge a grouse," he said quietly, "it's personal. You and him. For the grudge to be settled properly, the forms must all be followed. The grouse may be a sneaky rascal, an unmannered, lawless villain. But no matter how scornfully he's treated you, you must never stoop to his level. Oh, it's war to the death. But that death must be rendered with honor and respect, on the chosen field of battle, with the lines drawn and the boundaries clearly maked out and the weapons agreed upon. No other death will do. Do you see?"

I shrugged.

He reached into his game pocket and showed me how he had settled his grudge. Its eyes had once been beady and sly. But it wore fur, not feathers, and its ears and skinny tail were tipped with white, and I had no doubt that its intent had been evil.

"I caught it creeping on on *my* grudge bird," Doc grumbled. He stood up and stuffed the weasel back into his game pocket. "Let's get out of here. This season's over. Now I've got a whole year to properly nurse this grudge."

Part IV

Out of Season

I killed hundreds of ducks in my boyhood, yet as I strive to recall the circumstances it is not the plummet-like descent of their stricken bodies I see, nor do I hear in fancy the soul-stirring thud as they crash down upon the water. Memory paints, rather, a picture of the frost-browned grasses, with the sea wind stirring them into undulating motion, and the cloud shadows chasing one another interminably across them. I smell their salty sweet tang once more, and hear again the murmur of the distant ocean and the gentle lapping of the tide waters among the tules along the river bank.
—Burton L. Spiller
MORE GROUSE FEATHERS, 1938

Chapter 11

Confessions of a Reformed Crow Hunter

We usually see the crow on his worst behavior—hacking at the bloody carcass of a woodchuck beside the highway, skulking from the nest of a heartbroken song sparrow, or plucking corn seedlings from a farmer's field.

He looks evil and acts guilty, like a creature bent on making crime pay. He has a shiny black coat, shifty eyes, a cruel beak, and the scratchy, conspiratorial voice of a villain who drinks and smokes too much. In 1835 James Audubon said of the crow: "Almost every person has an antipathy to him, and scarcely one of his race would be left in the land, did he not employ all his ingenuity, and take advantage of all his experience, in counteracting the evil machinations of his enemies."

Upland Days

I used to shoot crows. I did it without antipathy, nor did my machinations seem evil to me at the time. Crow hunting was simply good, challenging sport. The fact that I could equate each crow I knocked out of the sky with a couple clutches of duck or songbird eggs or a few rows of a farmer's corn seemed to give purpose to the hunt. I didn't understand until later that it was a pitiful rationalization.

I hunted crows in May, exploiting their noblest instincts. I drove the back roads of my part of New England, stopping every few miles to hide the car under a low-branching tree. I wore camouflage clothing and crouched in the bushes at the edge of a clearing. Then I'd try to lure them in, mimicking on my reed call the plaintive cry of a fledgling crow in trouble.

The scout would answer from the distance, a rasping *caw* clearly saying, "I'm coming. Keep talking. Help is on the way."

I'd increase the insistence of my call. "Please hurry! I'm in big trouble here!"

A minute or two later, the scout would come cruising in, high and silent, his darting eyes searching below him. Then I had two choices: shoot the scout, or lay low and hope he didn't see me. If I managed to shoot him, the rest of the flock would come to see what had happened. But if the scout spotted me, or if I shot and

Confessions of a Reformed Crow Hunter

missed, he'd wheel away, barking a series of sharp, staccato notes: "Danger! Stay away! It's a trap!"

Ornithologists have since told me that he was probably saying a good deal more, because crows have a highly developed, complex language. "I found a man with shotgun!" that scout was crying. "It's the same guy who drove that Ford down the road a few minutes ago!"

When I managed to avoid being seen by the scout—and I failed more often than not, because crows have remarkable eyesight—he'd go back for the troops. I'd hear them off in the distance, debating the situation, a loud and emotional town meeting discussion, all of them talking at once. A few minutes later two dozen crows would come circling and swooping frantically overhead, hell-bent on rescuing their wayward baby, and then no amount of shotgun blasting could intimidate them. A young crow in trouble concerned the entire flock, and as I blasted away at them, it didn't occur to me to admire their courage and their concern—was it even something akin to love?—for each other.

Hunters have been the least of the crow's problems. Their eradication has been officially sanctioned in our nation's history. Government bounties prompted some citizens in Oklahoma in

1937, for example, to bomb a roost, killing 26,000 crows. In 1940, 328,000 crows were blasted from their roosts in Illinois. As early as 1835, Audubon reported that bounties had been paid for 400,000 crows in a single Midwestern state.

Americans have sprayed crows with poison gas from airplanes, baited them with arsenic-laced eggs and poisoned corn, and bombed them with shrapnel grenades and dynamite.

Our mindless plundering of the land has turned woodcock cover into shopping malls and highway cloverleafs. Maturing forests have made grouse habitat scarce, and the best efforts of well-meaning individuals and organizations to restore it feel futile and too late. The crow, meanwhile, has laughed raucously at our most earnest attempts to eliminate him. He has, ironically, prospered.

It shouldn't surprise us, though, for in nature the fittest survive, and the crow, above all, is fit. Naturalists dispute whether the crow does more harm than good, but they agree on one thing: The crow is just about the smartest critter on two wings.

Once, strolling through the spring woods, I heard the conversational jabbering of a flock of crows in the distance. I crouched down beside a bush and, without really attempting to hide, I squawked a crude imitation of a crow call with my own voice. To

Confessions of a Reformed Crow Hunter

my surprise, I received a reply, and moments later the entire flock came swarming overhead. I remained there, more or less in plain view, "talking" to them. They circled and dived near me, and several even perched in nearby trees—all within easy shotgun range.

I hurried home, hastily changed into my camouflage hunting shirt, and grabbed my shotgun and crow call. I snuck back into the woods, hid under some young hemlocks, and tried the reed call. This time they sent their scout. He came in low and fast, executed an abrupt turn, and fled back to his flock, crying a message that was perfectly clear to me: "That guy's back. But this time he's got a gun!"

Then I understood what Henry Ward Beecher meant when he said that if men wore feathers and wings, very few of them would be clever enough to be crows.

The crow's cleverness takes many forms. Even when I hunted them I knew they had an impressive vocabulary. I could imitate the young crow's "Help!," and I recognized the scout's "I'm coming" and "Danger!" Ornithologists have identified twenty-three distinct vocalizations, including calls for assembly, dispersal, distress, announcement, scolding, contentment, and mating. Crows sing special tunes in duet—surprisingly pleasant airs, in fact. They even have different words for each of their enemies: The caw meaning "owl" differs from the one for "hawk" or "guy with a shotgun."

The crow's ability to communicate reflects more than raw intelligence. After all, only a creature with highly developed social and cooperative habits *needs* the sophisticated language of the crow. I recognized that when I hunted them. The whole flock joined the rescue mission for the fledgling in trouble—a great extended family, all sharing responsibility for the well-being of each member.

Their scouts not only check the calls of the crow hunter, but they also seek out likely feeding grounds. When a flock of crows arrives to devastate a field of tender corn sprouts, you can be sure a scout has summoned them. And while others dine, one alert sentry remains perched atop the highest nearby tree to watch for approaching danger.

Crows also know that there's strength in numbers. A hawk or owl foolhardy enough to attack a crow soon finds himself assailed by a swirling, pecking mob. No wonder they call a flock of crows a "murder!"

The crow is more than a finely tuned bundle of instincts. He's also a problem solver. People have observed crows dropping

Confessions of a Reformed Crow Hunter

clams and nuts onto the highway for passing cars to run over and crush, then swooping down during a lull in the traffic to peck at the sweet insides.

Half a dozen different ice fishermen have sworn to me that they've been outfished by crows. Each fisherman's story is essentially the same: While tending his red-flagged tipups, he says, he became aware of a silent black specter watching him from the leafless branches of an old lakeside oak tree. For an hour or more the crow observed the man dash from his shelter to haul in the line each time a flag popped up. Finally, satisfied that he understood, and responding faster than the fisherman, the crow swooped down to the next tipped-up flag. He grabbed the line in his beak and marched back from the hole until the fish lay flopping on the ice. The canny bird then calmly pecked the flesh off his catch.

The official status of the crow shifted in 1972 when the federal government concluded a treaty with Mexico amending the 1936 Migratory Bird Treaty. Thenceforth, states were required to protect crows from hunters during their peak nesting seasons, and otherwise permit a maximum of 124 days of legal hunting. The crow thus achieved belated recognition as something more than a varmint—if, perhaps, still something less than a game bird.

Shooting crows is now forbidden at the time when they are most vulnerable—when their young are on the nest. The rest of the time the crow remains a cunning, cautious adversary for those who would try to shoot him. The same call that brings crows swarming during their nesting season will receive only a distant, derisive "fageddaboudit" for reply in August.

Federal regulations do allow exceptions in the case of depredation—plundering a cornfield, annoying livestock, or ravaging a henhouse. In such cases crows are fair game in any season.

Hunters grumble about "politics" and "big government" in response to such laws, although they might admit that crows deserve some sort of protection.

But they sure don't need it.

That the crow plays a more complex role in the ecological scheme of things than farmers and songbird lovers believe should come as no surprise. Crows are omnivorous, and there's the clue. Reviled as a predator, the crow actually performs two important functions: He weeds out the less fit of certain other species, and he preys on other predators. For example, the crow

Confessions of a Reformed Crow Hunter

is the number one enemy of the blue jay, itself a vicious plunderer of songbird eggs and chicks.

Consider the crow's other food sources. About twenty percent of the crow's diet consists of vegetation—corn seedling when available, sure, but plenty of other stuff besides. They'll gorge on whatever insects they can find. And since the crow prefers carrion above all else—not to mention the odd fish plucked from under an ice fisherman's nose—that leaves a relatively small part of his diet to songbird and duck eggs and nestlings.

The adult crow must consume nearly half of his body weight in food every day, so he turns up his beak at nothing edible. Whatever is abundant is what he'll eat. Songbird eggs in season, by all means. A field of newly sprouted corn, of course. But a cloud of locusts will bring many murders of crows to feast, too. June bugs, cutworms, or gypsy moths on the upswing of their cycle—all become grist for the crow's undiscriminating mill.

The crow is a crafty rascal. He's adaptable, pragmatic, inventive, and ubiquitous. He thrives comfortably in Death Valley, where the daytime temperature reaches 120°F, and in Canada with its 40°F-below-zero winters. You'll see him in city parks as well as in the wilderness.

Thoreau said of the crow, "This bird sees the white man come and the Indian withdraw, but it withdraws not. Its untamed voice is still heard above the tinkling of the forge. It sees a race pass away but it passes not away. It remains to remind us of aboriginal nature."

A century and a half after Thoreau wrote those words, the crow still remains, undaunted by highways and factories, cities and airplanes—as misunderstood now as he was in Thoreau's time.

The crow, like Rodney Dangerfield, still gets no respect. Yet he is, arguably, The American Bird, an apt symbol of all that is best—and worst—in our people. He's America's most complex and perhaps our most interesting bird, and I can no longer justify shooting at him. I can only urge would-be crow haters to heed Audubon's plea to ". . . reflect a little, and become more indulgent toward our poor, humble, harmless, and even most serviceable bird, the Crow."

Chapter 12

Jumping Black Ducks

Back in the '50s, when Art Currier and I were teenagers, our fathers shot black ducks the traditional, gentlemanly way, over decoys from a blind. Art and I didn't mind doing it that way. But we liked jumping them even better.

Jumping ducks from the tidal marshes in December was the next best thing to grouse and woodcock hunting. It involved the same sort of stealth and cunning, or at least we thought it did, and when we did it well, our reward was the sudden splashy flush of birds springing from a hidden pothole, ditch, or creek corner.

After the upland season closed, Art and I prowled the broad salt marshes on the Massachusetts north shore. A salt marsh is one of those blurry boundary places, a kind of breathing mem-

Upland Days

brane that filters life back and forth between sea and land. Marshes are laced with capillaries, veins, and arteries, and their creases, potholes, and creeks pulse with the ebb and flow of its tidal lifeblood.

We woke up in the dark so we could be creeping across the marsh just before dawn on a late-December morning, around the time when the stars were beginning to wink out overhead, and when out toward the horizon over the Atlantic Ocean, faint streaks of pink were just starting to bleed into the sky. The marsh grass was frozen brittle. It crunched underfoot, and the mud was icy-slick. Our gloved fingers gripping our shotguns quickly went numb, and so did our toes inside our hip boots. We spoke with whistles and hand signals, while Julie, Art's Springer, followed at heel, and in the vast silence we stopped often to listen for the soft gabble of black ducks paddling in the potholes and ditches. Each step might jump a duck—or a dozen or more of them.

At those magical times, a salt marsh is surely the most starkly, breathtakingly beautiful place on earth. Even as hard-hunting teenagers, Art and I always had the good sense to pause and take notice of it.

Jumping Black Ducks

Until the ponds and creeks froze over, we used a canoe to jump black ducks in swamps and brushy trout streams. But after the first hard freeze, we followed the ducks to the coast. There they traded back and forth between the marsh and the sea according to tide and wind and weather and time of day—and other mysterious factors known only to them. Typically they moved out of the marshes in the morning and came back to the winding creeks and hidden potholes around dusk.

Art and I liked to hit the marsh on mornings when low tide came around sunrise. The trick to jump-shooting ducks was to sneak up within shotgun range of them before they spotted us and panicked into flight. On a high tide, they were scattered all over the marsh, and with the water brimming at the tops of the banks, they could see us coming from a hundred yards or more.

Black ducks were alert and spooky. A grouse might hunker in a blowdown while you walked past him. Ducks always flushed the instant they saw or heard you.

The ebbing tide emptied the ditches and potholes and congregated the ducks in the corners and backwaters of the shallow creeks. At dead low tide, the high banks covered us so we could creep close.

Upland Days

At ground level, a marsh looks as flat as a prairie, a broad, undifferentiated expanse of sere, wind-bent marsh grass. But Art and I had our marshes all mapped out in our heads. We knew every twist and turn of every creek that wound through them.

We moved along about forty yards apart until we approached a creek bank. Then we went down on elbows and knees. That was Julie's signal to sit, and she'd wait while Art and I crawled forward, pausing now and then to listen for the conversational quacks and gabbles that told us we had ducks in front of us.

Sometimes, even when there was no way they could've seen us, one or two or twenty of them would jump from the creek before we'd snuck within shotgun range. Art and I would curse them, of course, but we admired their sharply tuned instincts. We figured black ducks were about the smartest birds on earth.

Back then, the limit was five blacks. I don't recall that Art or I ever limited out. But we did shoot a lot of ducks. When we managed to sneak up to the rim of the creek bank without spooking them, we whistled and hand-signaled, then stood up simultaneously. The air instantly filled with ducks. A few memorable times each of us knocked down a pair.

Julie was a marvelous retriever. She always went after the cripples first, and I don't remember her ever losing a duck.

Jumping Black Ducks

One particularly frigid morning toward the end of our hunt, we were working our way back to the car. The wind was driving hard kernels of snow into our faces and a strong tide was filling the creeks. We were carrying our guns at our sides, talking casually, when a pair of blacks jumped. Art nailed the one that broke in his direction. The other one beat for the sea off to my left. With thick gloves and numb fingers, I fumbled at the safety, and by the time I'd flicked it off, the duck was nearly out of range. I shouldn't have shot.

I thought I'd missed. The bird flew hard, a dim black shape quickly disappearing into the swirling snow. And then Julie was in the water, swimming against the heavy currents in the direction my duck had taken. Art yelled at her to fetch his bird, but she ignored him. I watched the duck I'd shot at, and just before I lost it in the driving snow, I thought I saw it falter, then begin angling downward.

"I might've hit that bird," I told Art.

"I hope to hell you didn't," he said. "It must be half a mile away by now."

He kept yelling into the wind for Julie, but she was gone.

Art's duck was circling in an eddy, stone dead, and he managed to retrieve it without going over his hipboots. When he came back, we squatted on the bank. I'm sure we were both thinking the same thing: Julie had a big heart, but she was only a little Springer spaniel, not really a water dog, and no match for the powerful tidal currents and the frigid water.

"I'm sorry," I said. "I should never have shot."

He nodded, and it was unclear whether he was forgiving me or agreeing with me.

We squinted into the wind and snow for more than half an hour. Finally Art stood up. "Well," he said, "looks like she's gone." He shook his head. I saw tears in his eyes, and I didn't think it was from the wind. "Stupid little mutt. Thinks she's some kind of—hey!"

We both saw her at the same time. Julie was trotting along the bank across the creek from us, looking for a place to cross. She was carrying a black duck in her mouth. The bird looked as big as a goose in the little dog's mouth.

Inevitably, the bulldozers came and gnawed away at the inland edges of our salt marshes. They leveled the scrubby hills that sloped down to the marsh and left hard-top roads and housing developments and No Trespassing signs behind. They didn't violate the marshes themselves, although we figured

Jumping Black Ducks

they eventually would once they figured out how to keep the tide out.

Art and I continued to jump-shoot black ducks on our north shore marshes. Creeping east over the frozen mud and brittle grass at sunrise on a December morning, we could almost fool ourselves into thinking nothing had changed.

But, of course, everything had changed, as it always does. Up and down the coast, civilization had pushed too close to the marshes and to black duck breeding habitat. Mallards interbred with blacks, further decimating their numbers.

We jumped fewer and fewer black ducks from our potholes and creeks. Those who count ducks reported that, by the 1980s, the Atlantic flyway black duck population had plummeted to a little over 200,000, down from around 500,000 in the 1950s, when Art and I began jumping them. The bag limit went from five blacks to four to two and then to just one a day. For us, it had always been academic. We rarely shot a limit when it was five, and when it was just two, we still didn't.

Art Currier and I are a lot older now than we were back when we were teenagers, when we thought our marshes would always

Upland Days
138

be filled with the gabbling of black ducks on a December morning. Now we know it'll never be the same. Nothing ever is.

These days we jump enough mallards to keep us going back to our marshes now and then. Mallards are not as wily as blacks. If black ducks are wild and spooky native brook trout, then mallards are dumb hatchery stockers—pale imitations. But we still love that magical time when fingers of pink begin clawing into the eastern sky and, overhead, the stars are winking out.

Occasionally a stray black jumps with a flock of mallards. Although a black duck could be mistaken for a female mallard when it's silhouetted against the eastern horizon at daybreak, Art and I know the difference. Black ducks spring off the water quicker and fly harder than any mallard.

We shot our last black duck about a dozen Decembers ago. We set it up the day before by telephone, the way we always did. Art's backyard stretches down to the banks of the Merrimack River in Newburyport. It's just a five-minute drive from there to several of the marshes we've been walking since we were kids. He gave me a tide and sunrise reading, and I told him he'd find me in his kitchen when he stumbled downstairs at 5:30, and the coffee better be ready.

Jumping Black Ducks

I heard an edgy eagerness in his voice. He'd been seeing lots of ducks trading back and forth from his back deck around sunrise, he said. Besides, he wanted to show Megan, his young Springer, what Julie had known. Julie had always been Art's favorite, and Megan was Julie's great-granddaughter. She reminded Art of Julie. She worked close, and had showed us a good nose for grouse and woodcock and a willingness to retrieve, but we'd never taken her to the marsh.

The sky was still black when I pulled into Art's driveway. His boots and shotgun and hunting coat were piled on the porch, and I found him sitting at his kitchen table cradling a mug of coffee. I went straight to the pot, poured myself a mugful, then leaned back against the counter. "Well," I said, "all set?"

When he looked up at me, I saw that his eyes were red. He opened his mouth to say something, then shook his head and took a sip of coffee. He cleared his throat, and his eyes seemed to be asking me for understanding.

"What's the matter?" I said.

"Megan," he whispered. "She got hit last night. A car. She—we had to put her down."

"Oh, man," I said. "I'm sorry." I sat down across from him. "Do you want to talk about it?"

Upland Days

140

"No," he said. "I want to go hunting."

"You sure?"

He nodded. "I've been thinking about it all night. It may sound stupid, but I think Megan would've wanted us to go."

It was still dark when we pulled off the road beside the marsh. We waited in the car, sipping coffee, until legal shooting time. Then we tugged on our hipboots, uncased our shotguns, loaded up, and started across the marsh.

The sky was pewtery gray under a heavy cloudbank, and a chill breeze was blowing in off the ocean. We hadn't gone fifty yards when a duck exploded from the twisting creek practically at Art's feet. I saw it all in slow motion—the big duck a dark silhouette pushing hard against the low sky, Art's gun slamming against his shoulder, moving with the duck, bucking when he pulled the trigger, the bird hesitating, then cartwheeling down a measurable second after the sound of the shot reached my ears.

"Good shot," I called. "Mallard?"

"Black," he said.

We both headed for where the bird had gone down, and we searched for an hour before we gave up. We figured the duck had landed in one of the creek's meanders and dived. Black ducks will do that.

Jumping Black Ducks

"Enough hunting for one day, huh?" I said.

He nodded, and we headed back across the marsh to the car. To this day, Art believes Megan would have found that duck.

One recent December morning Art and I found the marsh full of black ducks. It was as if every surviving black in the eastern flyway had decided to come back to our marsh, just to remind us of how it used to be.

We kept our shotguns dangling at our sides and watched them fly. Although we'd like to think that black ducks are on their way back, the statistics tell us otherwise.

We do not shoot them anymore, not even our one-bird limits. Nowadays, one black duck a day is too many to kill.

Chapter 13

Virtual Pheasants

According to the myth, Jason and the Argonauts, on one of their golden fleece expeditions, found ringneck pheasants on the banks of the Phasis River in Colchis, a country on the shores of the Black Sea. Jason brought some of these gaudy birds back to Greece with him, where they were given their scientific name, based on their legendary origin: *Phasianus colchicus*.

However they actually got there, these colorful natives of the Far East flourished in Greece. Their descendants were transported to Rome, thence to Europe, where pheasant hunting became the sport of the English nobility. Even before the invention of firearms, pheasants were hunted with crossbows and falcons. George Washington liberated a few ringnecks at Mount

Upland Days

Vernon, and several other subsequent efforts were made to introduce the birds into North America.

But it wasn't until the late 1800s that stocked pheasants survived and reproduced in the United States. By 1900 or so, they'd filled vacant ecological niches from coast to coast and became, arguably, as popular a quarry for bird hunters as ruffed grouse, woodcock, ducks or quail, our native game birds.

Ringneck pheasants were the brown trout of the American uplands.

I don't see wild pheasants much anymore, not the way I did forty years ago when I was a kid growing up in eastern Massachusetts. Back then, they were abundant in fields and woodsy edges and swamps and hedgerows. In the fall, after the cornfields had been cut, we often saw them prowling among the brown stubble and jabbing at leftover kernels. In the winter they crept into our suburban backyard to peck at the cracked corn that spilled from our bird feeders.

I hunted them, of course. All of us hunted pheasants in those days. When I was in high school, Art Currier and I and some of our chums met after school almost every October afternoon with

Virtual Pheasants

our shotguns and Bean boots and boxes of shells. There were plenty of farmers in our hometown, and none of them thought twice about giving permission for half a dozen teenage boys to shoot shotguns on their property.

We didn't have dogs to help us, so we marched abreast through the fields and corn stubble, and the birds scuttled ahead of us, for pheasants would rather run than fly. The trick was to corner them in the thickets at the end of the field, where they stopped running to hide. Then we took turns playing bird dog. One of us would break open his gun, empty it of shells, and lay it on the ground. Then he'd plow into the briars and blowdowns to flush out the birds. The pheasants would explode out of there cackling, big birds whose long tails made them seem twice as big as they were. They accelerated quicker and flew faster than they appeared to, and the tendency was to forget to lead them and shoot off their tails.

After we combed the fields, we'd chase the birds we'd flushed into the surrounding woods and swamps. Sometimes we found grouse and woodcock there, and we shot at them, too. Cottontails and squirrels were also fair game. We were hunters, not purists.

Upland Days

At the end of the afternoon, we'd stop back at the barn, and the farmer would grin and say, "Heard a lot of bangin'. Git some?"

And if we'd had some luck, we'd split our bag with our host, which would guarantee us a warm welcome the next time.

It's different now. Mostly there are housing developments and condominiums and shopping malls and highway cloverleafs and par-three golf courses where the meadows and woodlots of my childhood used to be. One by one, the old farmers yielded to the temptations of real estate developers, and those who are left post No Hunting signs around their property. Sometimes, if you ask politely, they might give you permission to hunt. Most of them no longer trust people with guns.

Many of the towns in the part of the world where I grew up have banned hunting entirely.

But there aren't many wild pheasants left anyway. Housing developments and condominium complexes and shopping malls and cloverleafs and golf courses make poor pheasant habitat. Housecats and skunks and raccoons and crows and hawks and coyotes—creatures that have adapted to suburban civilization—prey efficiently on pheasant eggs and newly hatched chicks.

Virtual Pheasants

Ringneck pheasants remain the most popular quarry for Massachusetts hunters. But the birds are no longer wild. They are raised in pens, and throughout the season they are released into the fifty-odd Wildlife Management Areas (our delightfully innocuous term for "public hunting grounds") across the Commonwealth—the way hatchery trout are stocked in our ponds and streams—for the specific purpose of providing sport for licensed hunters.

Some of these WMAs are classic pheasant habitat. The Division of Fisheries and Wildlife plants them with corn and leaves tangly edges and hedgerows. They are surrounded by boggy marshlands and swales, alder and poplar hillsides, and evergreen and oak forests.

But if you've ever hunted wild pheasants, you won't be fooled. Armies of hunters have beaten permanent paths through the marshes and swales, and they leave empty 12-gauge shotgun shells scattered on the ground like confetti after a parade. There's always a lot of camaraderie on a WMA. Dogs sniff strange dogs, and hunters on the way out pass along the rumors about how many birds were stocked that morning to the guys on the way in. The trick to hunting success at a WMA is to get there early, when there's still room in the parking lot.

Upland Days

It's canned hunting, designer hunting. A WMA feels like an artificial trout pond where you pay for the fish you catch by the pound. Pen-raised pheasants, like hatchery-raised brook trout, are not creatures of nature. They are not cagey or swift or smart. They are not survivors. They are raised to be "harvested," the wonderful politically correct Fish and Wildlife euphemism for "killed."

It's easy to shoot these pheasants without guilt. Their abundance, in fact, is directly proportional to the numbers of them that we kill. The more hunters who buy licenses and shoot pheasants, the more birds Fish and Wildlife can afford to raise and release for our hunting pleasure.

I hunt them because if I want to go hunting for a few afternoon hours the way I used to when I was in high school, a WMA is all there is in the forest of No Hunting and No Trespassing signs where I live.

I wouldn't think of visiting a WMA on a Saturday. But once in a while toward the end of a wet Thursday afternoon in November I find the parking lot at my local WMA empty. Burt and I work the thick edges where any pheasants that survived the morning onslaught have likely taken cover. Stocked pheasants don't like to run the way their wild ancestors used to. They'll sit for a pointing dog. Burt likes that, and I do, too.

Virtual Pheasants

When I kick one of them up, it doesn't seem to fly as fast as I remember, either. I'm a mediocre wingshot, but I rarely miss one of these birds.

Still, on those rare afternoons when dozens of bird dogs aren't crisscrossing every field and swale and when hunter-orange isn't the landscape's dominant color, I can sometimes delude myself into thinking that I'm hunting. After all, there are the birds and the good cover and the shotgun and the dog.

But the delusion never lasts. It's *not* hunting. Not really. It resembles hunting. But it's fake.

"Virtual hunting," I call it.

I hunted quail for the first time with Rick Boyer at a plantation in Georgia. We had grits and ham hocks and biscuits and gravy for breakfast, and then we waited on the veranda for Lyle, our guide, to fetch us in his Chevy pickup, which had two dog boxes in the bed and a gun rack in the cab and a Confederate flag flying from the antenna.

We bumped over dirt roads past blossoming peach trees and fields rioting in wildflowers. It was late February, still dead winter back home in New England. But here it was springtime, and it was glorious.

Upland Days

150

Lyle talked about auto racing and farming and bird dogs and catfish. He called us "sir," and when we asked him not to, he said, "Cain't help it, sir. It's how I was brung up."

He stopped by a field. He called it a "course." He let out the dogs while Rick and I pulled on our boots.

Lyle whistled. When we looked up, we saw that one of his setters was on point and the other was honoring her. It was classic, straight out of Nash Buckingham, and I felt somehow connected to the very roots of American bird hunting.

I'd seen bobwhite quail on Cape Cod, heard them whistle toward evening, but I'd never hunted them before. I knew they gathered in coveys, and when they flushed, it would be a vast confusion of what the stories always called "little brown bombshells." The trick was not to flock shoot.

Rick and I got our shotguns loaded. Lyle motioned for us to move into position on either side of the dogs. He'd go in and kick up the birds, which apparently were hiding in a thicket of briars.

There were just two quail. One flew left, my way, rather more slowly than I'd expected, and the other went straightaway in front of Rick. I swung and shot and my bird dropped. Rick dumped his, too. It was vaguely disappointing. I'd expected a covey, swift fliers, pandemonium.

Virtual Pheasants

But it was Southern quail shooting, and I'd hit the first one I'd shot at over classic pointing dogs within minutes of arriving at the course.

By the time we'd stuffed our birds into our game pockets, the dogs were pointing again.

Lyle kicked up two more quail. Rick and I dropped both of them, too.

We followed beaten-down paths through the grass-and-briar course while the dogs worked the thick stuff, and every fifty yards or so they pointed, Lyle flushed, and we shot. The birds came mostly in pairs, and they flew straight, and Rick and I rarely missed.

When we came to the end of the course, Lyle muttered, "Twenty-two, right?"

"I wasn't counting," said Rick.

"Well, sir, I'm pretty sure we flushed twenty-two," said Lyle. "We got us a couple more somewheres." He scratched his head for a moment, then nodded. "This way, gentlemen," he said.

We followed him to a corner of the course that we had missed. Lyle called over the dogs, and a minute later they were pointing again.

Two more quail in our pockets.

Upland Days

152

The man really knows his cover, I was thinking.

Back at the truck, Rick and I unloaded our game pockets and laid nineteen birds on the ground. Lyle said we'd flushed twenty-four.

I'd never shot more than five birds—a woodcock limit—in one day in my life. That had cost me a box of shells. Today I'd shot ten in three hours, and I still had a fistful of shells left from the box I'd dumped into my pockets.

Sometime around then I figured it out.

While Rick and I had been eating the first grits of our lives that morning, Lyle was at our morning's course planting the two dozen quail we'd bought. He tucked the birds' heads under their wings and rocked them dizzy so they'd stay put, then set them out two by two, a pair under this hussock of grass, another pair in this briar tangle, another under this shrub—the same places, no doubt, where he'd put them out the day before for some other pair of Yankee shotgunners.

Southern "plantation hunting" is the private, upscale equivalent of a Massachusetts WMA—pen-raised birds and groomed terrain, all designed for the shooting enjoyment of anyone who can afford it.

Rick, of course, understood all this. He'd made the arrangements. He knew that we were paying about eight dollars for

Virtual Pheasants

every quail that was planted for us, whether or not we shot it. "We could have had chukars or pheasants," he said, "but they run twenty dollars apiece. I figured we'd go for more bang for the buck."

It was a lot like learning my father was Santa Claus. I'd like to report that my disillusionment was so complete that I packed my bags and flew back into the New England winter.

But I didn't. I stayed out the week and enjoyed the Southern cooking, the Southern hospitality, the Southern springtime. The dog work was spectacular and, of course, we got to do a lot of shooting. In the end, my disappointment that the birds weren't wild was neutralized by the knowledge that shooting dozens of them had no more impact on the fragile natural balance of things than buying a shrink-wrapped chicken in a supermarket.

Lyle told us that wild coveys of quail were so scarce and hard to find in the South these days that few people hunted them anymore. When I told him that this plantation hunting seemed fake, he shrugged. "In the old days," he said, "when the birds were wild, the old plantation owners grew crops and cut and burned the fields for them. They knew where all the coveys were, and they only let their friends hunt 'em. It wasn't all that much different. They raised 'em for hunting back then, too. This here's what we got for bird hunting nowadays."

Upland Days

154

Virtual hunting. It takes only a few minor adjustments in your thinking to call it, simply, hunting.

It's the future.

Virtual hunting needs some fine-tuning. In its public forms such as the Massachusetts WMA, there are too many hunters chasing too few birds over not enough acres of not very wild terrain. No one who has scouted the New England countryside for grouse and woodcock covers, and hoarded the gems he's discovered, can take much pleasure from that.

Even on expensive private hunting areas, where they put out more birds and give you your own course to hunt, pen-raised pheasants and quail are stupid and poor flyers.

Pheasant farmers, I understand, are developing hybrid pheasants, smaller, swifter birds that give hunters a greater wingshooting challenge. This matters little to me. If the main point of bird hunting was target shooting, I'd give up birds entirely and shoot skeet or sporting clays.

So far, thankfully, no one has been able to raise ruffed grouse or woodcock in captivity.

Every fall Art Currier, in celebration of his own birthday, organizes a day of pheasant hunting for himself and several of his

Virtual Pheasants

friends. Some of us have hunted and fished since we were kids. Others take to the woods only once a year, on Art's birthday hunt.

Because this is a special occasion, a once-a-year celebration of autumn, we spend the day at a hunting preserve, sort of a private WMA, a Northern plantation where we are assured of finding birds and privacy.

Over the years, we have sampled a number of New England hunting preserves. We haven't found much difference among them. We pay a per-man fee, which guarantees that a prescribed number of pheasants will be put in the fields for us. On the morning of our arrival, one of the preserve's guides slips into the assigned fields and plants the birds, which have been rocked with their heads tucked under their wings so they will not fly or run away before we hunters get there.

Then we are divided into groups of three and directed to our appointed fields. We know six pheasants have been deposited there. If they are still there, and if the dogs do their jobs, we will get some shots and perhaps bag a few pheasants.

I always enjoy the comradeship of Art's day. I enjoy watching the dogs work, and shooting an occasional pen-reared pheasant does not give me the twinge of regret that I get when I shoot a wild bird.

Upland Days

156

Because we have the place to ourselves, it's more fun than a WMA, although I never confuse a day on a preserve with real hunting. But before I visited Hidden Meadow Farm in Temple, New Hampshire, I assumed that the canned hunting-preserve "chicken shoot," as Keith calls it, was, for better or for worse, bird hunting's only future, and I had better get used to it.

Marty Connolly, who owns Hidden Meadow, has a different idea. He regularly releases pen-raised pheasants on his dairy farm and on several other area farms that he leases. Before they are hunted, these birds have time to become acclimated to the terrain, to discover food sources and hiding places, and to hone their survival instincts. Those that manage to evade hawks and coyotes soon acquire all the characteristics of wild birds. There's evidence that some of them live long enough to reproduce.

Hunters at Hidden Meadow pay a flat rate for a day's hunting. Marty guarantees only that there are birds somewhere in the woods and fields and that you'll have the place to yourself. Good hunters with talented dogs can bag a lot of pheasants. But they can also get skunked. The terrain is varied and natural and rugged—old farmland, boggy swamps, oak ridges, brambly edges, weed-grown meadows. Marty and his sons cut it and plant it to

Virtual Pheasants

give the birds food and cover. There are no beaten footpaths in these pheasant farms.

It's very much like the way real hunting used to be. For a hunter, it's a superior alternative to both public hunting on WMAs and the sterile artificiality of the standard private hunting preserve.

But for Marty Connolly, Hidden Meadow offers more than just a good day of hunting for folks like Art Currier and his friends. Marty thinks it's a model for what could be the salvation of the Yankee farmer.

Family farms, once the backbone of the New England economy, are disappearing at an alarming rate. Our hilly rock-bound terrain and sterile, acidic soil simply cannot produce enough to enable farmers to make ends meet. Old farms are being sold or taken in lieu of unpaid taxes. They are transformed into housing developments, shopping malls, highway cloverleafs, and golf courses.

In many cases, they are simply abandoned and left to grow to the mature forest that makes such poor wildlife habitat.

All of them could be turned to profit, and so remain part of our New England landscape, simply by stocking them with game birds, cutting and planting them to provide forage and habitat, and opening them to controlled pay-as-you-go hunting. Marty calls this "agricultural wildlife management." Naturalized pheasants are the "crop," equivalent to chickens or corn or apples. The farmer manages his land to maximize his crop's quality and yield, and hunters pay him for the opportunity to harvest it. It works just like the strawberry or apple grower who invites people in to pick their own.

Marty points out that the agricultural wildlife management concept, besides giving bird hunters a reasonable facsimile of old-time pheasant hunting, simultaneously provides a number of other benefits: Land managed for game birds also offers ideal habitat for grouse, woodcock, turkeys and deer, not to mention songbirds and other wild creatures; local businesses such as motels and restaurants are boosted by visiting hunters; farmers' income from hunting subsidizes traditional agricultural activities such as dairy and truck farming; and family farming might once again be an integral and profitable part of the New England culture and economy. Agricultural wildlife management also provides places where youngsters can be safely introduced to hunting, and thus the hunting tradition may be perpetuated.

Agricultural wildlife management might become the new, improved New England version of the Southern quail-hunting plantation.

Virtual Pheasants

Marty Connolly and a growing cadre of supporters are fighting anti-hunting propagandists and entrenched political interests as they try to make the concept an option for all New England farmers. Meanwhile, some of us flaunt his bumper stickers, which read: BAG A PHEASANT, FEED A COW, KEEP NEW HAMPSHIRE GREEN.

If virtual hunting is the future of our sport, as seems likely, then maybe Marty's got the right idea.

Chapter 14

Sea Duck Weather

The alarm jangles at 4:00 A.M. I fumble for it, turn it off, sit up, then collapse back onto my pillow, hoping to recapture a dream.

A few minutes later Keith scratches at my door. "I know you're still snoozing," he hisses.

"I'm up," I lie.

"Get moving. It looks like a great day."

I crawl out of bed. The floor feels like ice under my bare feet, which motivates me. I tug on my wool socks and insulated long johns, and then I add layers—wool pants, wool shirt, wool sweater. The five-mil neoprene chest-high waders and the hooded camouflage parka and wool gloves will go on later.

Upland Days

162

I stumble downstairs. Keith's kitchen is warm and smells of freshly brewed coffee and woodsmoke.

He's pacing. "Let's *go*," he says.

I peer out the window. The sun won't rise for another three hours. It's the darkest time of the night.

But I can read the thermometer. The red column stands about an inch tall. "It's minus two out there," I report.

"Perfect," he says. "Ready?"

We lug our shotguns and shell boxes and thermoses of coffee out to the driveway where the truck and trailered boat wait for us. We'd hitched it up and loaded the dekes the night before.

Keith's duck boat is an L. L. Bean model—shaped more or less like a big, broad-beamed canoe. With camouflage netting hung over its removable aluminum skeleton, it's a floating blind. Two or three men can hide in it and shoot comfortably. Its camouflage paint job provides us with our ongoing joke.

I look around. "Where's the boat?"

"Ha, ha," Keith grumbles.

The air shoots icicle darts down my lungs. High in the black, naked trees a Northeast wind is already wheezing. "Oh, perfect," says Keith. "We got ourselves some weather."

Sea Duck Weather

It's December 31, the day of our traditional end-of-the-year Casco Bay sea-duck hunt, and it promises, in fact, to be a perfect day for it. A heavy cloudbank hangs low in the sky, and the moist, frigid wind promises more snow.

Duck hunters call it "weather." Most people call it "bad weather."

Weather keeps the ducks moving. The worse it is, the better. An old-fashioned New England ice storm is good. Wind and swirling snow is best of all. Good weather is bad, and vice versa, for sea-duck hunting.

A half hour and one stop at Dunkin Donuts later, Keith backs the boat down the ramp. I pull on my neoprene waders, slosh in up to my hips, and grab the painter when the boat slides off the trailer. The sea water is significantly warmer than the air.

We load the boat and head across the bay to the islands and rockpiles that cluster out there in the dark. Keith knows the way. I huddle in the bow, hugging my hands in my armpits. "Wind'll be bad coming back in," Keith shouts over the drone of the outboard.

"Pretty bad now," I observe, as we bounce over the chop, getting sprayed every time we crash down into a trough. The front of Keith's parka is sheeted with ice. "Good, I mean."

Upland Days

164

The sky is changing from black to gray by the time the jumbled rockpile alongside one of the small islands looms in front of us. Keith knows the tides and the bottom contours of Casco Bay, so I let him plot our strategies. Low tide has stranded us on a mud flat only once. I enjoy reminding Keith about that.

We spread the decoys so that they will bring the ducks into shotgun range when we anchor our boat against the rocks. The narrow passage between the islands will funnel the birds over our dekes—at least, that's the plan.

We rig the camouflage around the boat, slide our shotguns from their cases, set the shell boxes within reach, then pour coffee.

The sky is dull pewter under the clouds. Pellets of hard snow rattle off the hood of my parka. It sounds like birdshot.

Keith checks his watch. "Six-thirty," he announces. We have fifteen minutes to legal shooting time, which is a half hour before sunrise.

I hold my mug in one gloved hand and a donut in the other. The coffee is cold. The donut is frozen solid. That always happens. But the Dunkin Donuts stop is part of our ritual.

"Hey!" hisses Keith.

Sea Duck Weather

I follow the jut of his chin and see a string of ducks against the horizon. They are flying fast and low, no more than three feet over the water. "Eiders," says Keith, and I know better than to question him, although they are just black specks to my eye.

They cross a hundred yards out, then make a wide circle and come back, bearing down on our decoys. Now I can see that they are indeed eiders, eight of them.

"What time is it?" I ask.

"Too early. Let 'em go."

They flare at the decoys within easy shotgun range and veer away.

"Bang-bang," whispers Keith. "Go fetch."

The sky remains dark all morning. Snow blows horizontally across the sea. Decoys and duck boat rock in the chop. The wind stabs frozen knives through our bodies.

But it doesn't matter. When the ducks are flying, as they usually are on the last day of the year on Casco Bay, it's easy to ignore the weather. We see scoters and scaup, eiders and old squaw, and they all fly fast and low. When we shoot, we can sometimes see our pellets spray the water behind our targets. We've done this before. We are always amazed at how fast they fly.

Upland Days

166

The first time Keith took me sea-duck hunting, he said, "You've got to lead these birds about twice as much as you think. They really move."

I shrugged. Compared to drawing a bead on the darts and twists of grouse and woodcock in thick cover, I figured straight-fliers would be easy.

Soon a string of eiders materialized out of the gray horizon. We watched them veer toward our decoys. They were skimming over the water, and when they were about forty yards out, Keith whispered, "Now."

I picked the lead duck, swung hard—and dropped the fifth bird back.

"Nice shot," said Keith. "That's the one I would've gone for, too."

Some people call eiders "flying pillows." The image is all wrong. Over open water and under a full head of steam, eiders fly about 70 mph, which translates to more than 100 feet per second. I've never seen a pillow move that fast.

I've done the math. A charge of shot with a muzzle velocity of 1000 feet per second takes one-eighth of a second to travel forty yards. Between the time I pulled the trigger and my shotstring arrived, the ducks had flown twelve feet, which explains why my

Sea Duck Weather

puny two-foot lead hit the eider that was ten feet aft of my target.

Keith had been inviting me to hunt sea ducks with him for several years. I kept turning him down, citing the same reason that I quit hunting crows: I won't shoot anything that I can't eat, and I knew that sea-duck meat was inedible. I'd tried it once. It was a bad experience.

Finally Keith said, "You probably won't shoot one anyway. You've got to be a good wingshot to hit a sea duck."

"Now just a minute . . ."

"Look," he said. "I eat them. So if you should make a mistake and kill one, just give it to me. It won't go to waste."

"You don't, like, make your kids eat them, do you?"

"They love 'em. You just gotta know how to cook 'em."

So I compromised my principles and began hunting sea ducks. I turned over any birds I managed to shoot to Keith, and I resisted several threats and bribes before he finally persuaded me to sit down to a meal of sea duck, cooked his way.

"This is practically edible," I said. In fact, it was delicious. "How'd you do it?"

He told me. It sounded easy.

"That was a mistake, pal," I said. "From now on, I'm keeping all the ducks I shoot."

We have our limits—seven birds apiece—by ten o'clock, and we're huddled by the woodstove in Keith's kitchen by noon. We've had "good" weather and good hunting, and we've reassured ourselves that we are hardy fellows indeed. Anyone who can survive a day of sea-duck hunting, we tell each other, can surely survive whatever challenges another year might bring.

What I love about sea-duck hunting is how virtuous I feel afterward.

I'm not one of those wild-game gourmet cooks. But in this case, knowing how to convert sea ducks into something palatable—if not downright tasty—makes the difference between going hunting and staying home on a miserable winter's morning.

So here's the recipe:

Keith's Practically Edible Sea Duck

Sea ducks should be prepared the day before you intend to serve them, as you need to marinate the meat for about 36 hours.

Sea Duck Weather

1. Remove the breasts and discard the rest of the ducks. Keith once tried to convince me to try the legs. It was a bad idea. One eider breast feeds two. With smaller ducks such as old squaw, figure one breast per person.
2. Slice the meat off the breasts. The slices should be about one-quarter-inch thick.
3. Spread the breast slices in a high-sided platter and cover with milk. Cover with aluminum foil and marinate in the refrigerator all day, for about 12 hours. The evening before your feast, drain off the milk, rinse the meat, pat it dry on paper towels, then marinate again in fresh milk overnight, 8 to 12 hours. The two rounds of milk marinade will neutralize the objectional (that's my polite word for it), gamy flavor of sea ducks.
4. The morning before you plan to serve it, drain off the milk, rinse and pat dry again, and cover the meat with a robust red wine. Let it marinate in the refrigerator for 6 or 8 hours.
5. Drain the meat and pat it dry with paper towels. Do not rinse it this time.
6. Rub both sides of the meat with salt, freshly ground black pepper, ground red pepper, and dried sage and rosemary.

7. Sear the meat on both sides in a very hot skillet. Do not overcook. It should be rare on the inside.
8. Serve with cranberry sauce or chutney, wild rice, fresh green vegetables (steamed asparagus would be my choice, but it's not in season in New England in the winter), a green salad, and an excellent red wine.

Chapter 15

The Year They Opened the Season on Robins

It was a steamy afternoon in the middle of August, and thunderstorms were threatening when Doc, my gunning partner, came banging on my door. "Open up," he yelled. "Gimme a beer. I got news."

I took one look at him. His eyes were wide and his sparse white hair looked like a backlash. He was waving a piece of paper in the air. "Oh, oh," I said. "I see you got another bee up your butt. What is it this time?"

"Beer," he croaked. "I need a beer."

I fetched us a couple of beers and led Doc out onto the screen porch. He took the rocking chair, gulped down half his beer,

Upland Days

started jiggling his leg, then shoved the piece of paper he was clutching at me. "You seen this?" he said.

"You're rocking so fast it's a blur," I said. "What in hell is it?"

"This year's migratory bird regs, son. Seen 'em?"

"I glanced at them," I said. "Noticed they've cut back the woodcock season again."

Doc rolled his eyes. "Woodcock," he grumbled, as if it were a dirty word. He thrust the paper at me. "Here, take a look. Near the top, there, right above snipe."

Doc was rocking so fast I thought he was going to propel himself through the screen. I reached out and managed to snatch the paper from him. I smoothed it out on my leg and looked.

Then I began laughing.

"What's funny?" said Doc.

"It lists robins," I said.

"Exactly."

"Well," I said, "that's funny. That's *very* Goddamn funny. Open season on robins? I mean, let's go robin hunting, huh? Got your robin gun all oiled up? What kind of loads do you like for robins? You prefer a pointing robin dog or a flusher? Will your robin dog retrieve, or does it point dead? Hey," I said,

The Year They Opened the Season on Robins

barely able to contain myself, "what about finding some new robin covers?"

Doc stopped rocking and grabbed my arm. "Those are all excellent questions, young feller. We've got to ponder those questions."

I wiped the tears out of my eyes and looked at him. "You aren't the slightest bit serious, are you?"

"Serious?" he said. "Sure I'm serious. I'm dead serious!"

"Come on," I said. "We're talking about *robins*, for heavens sake. Robin redbreast, you know? The early bird. The puller of worms. The herald of spring. Who killed cock robin? I said the sparrow, with my twelve-gauge—"

"Dammit," he said, "pay attention. Robins are *game* birds. By definition. It says so right there. Season opens October twentieth and closes November twentieth. Five-bird daily limit, ten-bird possession limit. Cocks only."

I rolled my eyes. "Cocks only. I love it."

"It's a whole new sport," said Doc. "Think about it. We're gonna be pioneers, you and me. We'll write the definitive book. *Robin Hunting in North America.* We'll be famous."

"Wait a minute," I said. "You're the same guy who got all excited about hunting starlings and English sparrows a few years ago, right?"

He waved his hand dismissively. "Not the same thing at all. Starlings and English sparrows are varmints. No closed season, no bag limit. Besides, starlings taste lousy, and English sparrows won't sit for a pointing dog. But robins? Robins are game birds. It says so right there."

"You . . . um . . . ate a starling?"

"Of course. You don't think I'd shoot anything I wouldn't eat, do you? Now your robin, on the other hand . . . dark-breasted, probably. Like woodcock. Both eat worms. Broil 'em with that nice barbecue sauce of yours, robust red wine, wild rice, fresh greens . . ."

"Look," I said gently, "I hate to be the one to break the news to you, but this"—I slapped the piece of paper with the back of my hand—"is obviously a mistake. A typographical error, a misprint of some kind."

Doc drained his beer and pushed himself out of his chair. "Rules are rules, my boy. I figure we got a little less than eight weeks to find ourselves some good robin covers. I'm gonna go check my topo maps right now."

The next morning, while sipping my coffee on the back deck, I glanced up from my newspaper and spotted a cock robin tug-

The Year They Opened the Season on Robins

ging on a worm beside the birdbath. I thought of Doc and, chuckling to myself, I got up from my chair and started walking toward the bird.

He tilted his head at me, hesitated, gave the worm a quick tug, then suddenly let go and took off. He angled sharply over the perennial garden, darted behind the garage, and the last I saw of him was a gray-and-orange blur dipping over the stockade fence into the neighbor's yard.

I glanced around to make sure nobody had been watching me. When that robin flushed, my left hand had come up in front of me and my right hand had slapped against my jaw and my trigger finger had twitched. The word "Mark!" had risen in my throat.

I had to admit it: I would've missed.

Not only that. His flight had been utterly silent. He didn't roar like a grouse or whistle like a woodcock or cackle like a cock pheasant.

It occurred to me that in thick cover, a man could be proud to drop a flying robin.

When I got to the office that morning, I called my friend Ralph Perry at the Division of Fisheries and Wildlife. "Ralph," I said, "you've seen this year's migratory bird regulations, I assume?"

He blew a long sigh into the telephone. "Not you, too," he said.

"This robin thing," I said. "It's not for real, is it?"

"Hey," he said, "don't blame me. My phone hasn't stopped ringing for a week. I got PETA on my ass bigtime, plus Audubon, of course, and a bunch of Girl Scouts from East Boston, not even to mention the DAR and the Knights of Columbus and Senator Kennedy's office. I mean, East Boston? I don't think they even have grass in East Boston."

"I wasn't blaming anybody," I said.

"Blame the feds," he said as if he hadn't heard me. "Apparently some anti-hunting Congressman from California slipped a rider into an environment bill. Got robins added to the list of legal migratory game birds, figuring it'd gum up the works, delay the publication of the regs. Without regs, there'd be no laws, and without any laws, there'd be no legal hunting. At least, that's what this nut figured."

"He was wrong, huh?" I said.

"Yup. The regs got published and promulgated, and they list robins, and now me and my counterparts in the forty-nine other

The Year They Opened the Season on Robins

states have got our butts on the line. Typical of the feds. Make a mess and leave it up to the states to clean up after them." He sighed. "Anyway, I tell everybody the same thing."

"What do you tell them?"

"I tell them it's just a typical Washington blunder, a colossal boner, and it'll be corrected next year, so no harm done."

"Did you say *next* year?"

"Well, yeah. Too late to change the law now. But don't worry. Nobody's gonna shoot robins."

"I wasn't worried," I said.

A couple of weeks later Doc called. "I been doing some research," he said. I could practically hear his leg jiggling. "Did you know the robin's Latin name is *Turdus migratorius?*"

"*Turdus?*"

"Well, never mind," he said. "Reason I called, I got good news and bad news."

"Gimme the bad news first."

"The bad news is, my setter ain't gonna do the job on robins."

"How come?"

"He won't pay any attention to them. Remember how hard I worked breaking him from chasing stink birds? Well, for once, the training paid off. I took him out, found lots of birds, and all he'd do was point damn woodcock."

"Woodcock? Where?"

"The good news," he said quickly, "is, I found some terrific robin covers."

"You could've started in my backyard," I said. "They love our birdbath."

"Well, yeah, that's good," he said, "except you can't shoot firearms within a hundred fifty feet of a highway or—"

"Or five hundred feet of a dwelling," I said. "I know. I was joking, for God's sake."

"It's not a joking matter," he growled. "Anyway, what I learned about robins is that they like field edges and moist, alkaline soil. And you mentioned your birdbath. Very astute. They gotta have water to bathe in. And worms. They eat bugs and grubs and caterpillars and stuff, too, but they love worms. Just like what other favorite game bird?"

"Other?"

"Right. Woodcock. *Ergo*, I figured, where there are woodcock, we oughta find robins. So I scouted some of our old woodcock covers. You shoulda seen it. The ground was covered with chalking."

The Year They Opened the Season on Robins

"Chalking, huh?"

"Yep. The robin has a characteristic chalking. Firmer and grayer than a woodcock, easily distinguished."

"You find any woodcock?"

"Yeah, but I wouldn't worry about that. These places are loaded with robins. A scattering of local birds, plus it looks like the early flights are already coming in. Thing is, we gotta get us a robin dog. No time to retrain the setter, I'm afraid. So I was thinking, my niece has got a young cocker bitch, only goes out on a leash, ain't even housebroke. *Tabula rasa,* you might say. No prior training to break her of. I bet she'll go after robins. Whaddya think?"

"Cockers were originally woodcock dogs," I said. "That's how they got their name."

"Well, maybe," said Doc. "But I think we can break her from woodcock and make her into a helluva robin dog. I already talked to my niece."

"You told her you were gonna hunt robins?"

"Don't be ridiculous. I told her I'd housebreak her little cocker."

"You planning to paper-train her?"

"The point is," he said, "I'm going to train her on robins. So you can leave everything up to me. Just be ready to go bright and early on the twentieth."

"That's opening day for woodcock, too, you know."

"Forget the damn woodcock," said Doc. "We're going robin hunting." He paused. "It was pretty interesting," he said quietly.

"What was?"

"Those birds sit close. Don't run at all. They'd be a lot of fun with a pointing dog. And they fly surprisingly hard. At angles, you know? I mean, not as fast as doves or grouse, and not all corkscrewy like woodcock. But plenty tricky. And another thing—"

"They don't make any noise," I said.

"You noticed!" he said. "Imagine the challenge of shooting a bird you can't even hear in thick cover. There's nothing quite like it. It's a whole new sport."

I found myself smiling. "A whole new sport."

"So anyway," Doc said, "I'll pick you up the usual time on the twentieth. Bring that sweet little twenty-eight-gauge side-by-side of yours. Skeet loads, I'd say. You'll need plenty of shells."

"Now, listen—"

The Year They Opened the Season on Robins

"No insult intended, my boy. Those robins are sporty, that's all."

"Doc," I said, "the twentieth is a Friday. I know you retired senior citizens don't care what day of the week it might be, but I've got to work."

"You telling me you're gonna miss opening day of the first robin season in history?"

"I'm afraid I've got to."

"Where are your priorities, son?" he sighed. "Well, okay, then. I'll just have to hunt Opening Day alone. I'll break in my niece's cocker, get the lay of the land, and we'll slay 'em on Saturday. I'll call you Friday night with a report."

I was standing beside the telephone on the evening of October 20 dry-mounting my little 28-gauge double when the phone jangled. I snatched it up on the first ring.

"Well?" I said.

"Bad news," said Doc. "They're gone."

"Gone?"

"Yeah." He blew out a long breath. "Nothing but a bunch of woodcock. Not a robin anywhere."

Upland Days

"What do you think happened?"

"I figure all the flights went through. Shoulda known, all those birds in September."

"Nuts," I said.

"I been thinking," said Doc. "I figure this was some kind of malicious joke. Hell, they oughta know the migratory habits of robins before they set the season. I'm gonna write 'em a letter, remind them that here in New England the robins migrate in September, so October's too late. They should open on September first, like snipe."

"The covers were full of woodcock, though, huh?"

"Yeah, but don't worry about that. The woodcock flights won't be down in September to bother us next year. One good thing. The little cocker worked beautifully. Ignored all those damn woodcock. So next year—"

"I got an idea," I said.

"Don't start on the woodcock," said Doc.

"No, no," I said. "I'm thinking about robins. I read somewhere that in New England we have some native, nonmigratory birds. Not many people know that. They like evergreens and swamps. Places that don't freeze up. They hang around all winter. That first robin of spring? Native bird. That's what I read. Maybe it's

The Year They Opened the Season on Robins

too late to find any flight birds. But I bet we could scare up a few natives."

"Swamps!" said Doc. "Evergreens! That's brilliant. Secret robin covers for native birds after the flights have gone through. I got a couple places in mind already. I'll pick you up at seven."

"I'll be ready."

"It's gonna be tough hunting, sonny."

"I wouldn't want it any other way," I said.

Part V

Last Hunt

We were hunting Forgotten Land. It had been a settlement once, a century or more ago. There was evidence that the land had been cleared, but the forest had crept back and now all but hid the once fertile fields. Scattered about over the many hundreds of acres, were many almost obliterated cellar holes, and occasionally one came across the rotting remains of a crude farm wagon. Thoughts of the former occupants of the land kept intruding upon my mind. With the sweat of their brows they had wrested this soil from the clutch of the forest. With infinite exertion they had built their homes on the sunny slopes. They had lived and loved and died and were dust again. Dust! Their homes were dust, and timber was growing in the once fallow fields.

It was a cheerless place in which to hunt, but there were hundreds of wild apple trees scattered about and it was good grouse country.

—Burton L. Spiller
GROUSE FEATHERS, 1935

Chapter 16

Heartbreak 1963

Nick cradled his father's open shotgun across his lap. He was sitting on the ground with his back against a dead oak tree drinking black coffee from the steel cup that screwed onto the top of his thermos. The sun was high and yellow in the pale November sky, and the air was too thin to hold any warmth. The steel cup warmed his hands, and steam rose from the coffee.

He gazed out at the meadows and low wooded hills that sloped down to the big salt marsh. His father had called this place Heartbreak. The shotgun was a 20-gauge double with two triggers, a Winchester Model 21, and Nick had always shot it well. He didn't know why his father called the place Heartbreak. It was a strange name for such a beautiful place, and it was where

Upland Days

188

the old man had always come to find peace when things were bothering him. He had died a year and two months earlier without ever explaining the name.

Nick lifted the cup to his lips, blew on it, took a sip. It was black and bitter, the way he liked it. "Men take it black," the old man used to say. Nick's father had taught him to drink coffee. He wasn't sure how old he'd been. No more than seven or eight. He'd crawled out of bed when he heard the alarm go off at four o'clock on a frigid December morning and went down to the kitchen to watch the old man assemble his duck-hunting gear.

The kitchen had been warm, and it smelled of freshly brewed coffee and wet bird dog. Outside, it was still nighttime, and the light from the kitchen window was orange on the snow. Nick had huddled in the breakfast nook, and his old man had put a mug of coffee in front of him. "Drink it," he'd said.

It had burned his tongue and tasted bitter, but Nick drank it. Nick had always obeyed his old man.

His mother had told Nick to take anything of his father's that he wanted. "Take those damn books," she'd said. "Take the paintings, the fishing rods, the guns, the boots and shirts and smelly foul-weather gear. Take whatever you want. I don't want to look at his old junk anymore."

Heartbreak 1963

Nick took the Model 21. He told his mother she could get rid of everything else.

He hadn't planned to hunt today. Nobody had expected this Monday to be a national holiday. It never had been before, and Nick guessed it never would be again. He had spent the weekend watching Huntley and Brinkley on his black-and-white television. He'd turned it on when he got home from work on Friday afternoon—they'd let everybody go early—and he hadn't turned it off until he'd left his apartment this morning. He had not turned on the car radio during his drive to Heartbreak. He'd heard enough.

A string of leafless oak trees ran along the ridgeline of the low hills beyond the meadow a mile off to his right. A murder of crows sat in their topmost branches. From where Nick was sitting, the crows were black specks against the washed-out sky, but their conversational caws carried clearly through the thin air. He figured they were discussing the weather. What had happened in Dallas over the weekend didn't affect crows.

It was all politics, Nick told himself. It shouldn't affect him, either.

He and his father used to hunt crows in May when their young were fledglings and they sometimes flopped out of their nests and got lost or were attacked by hawks. They'd hide the old

Upland Days

man's Cadillac under the low boughs of a big pine tree, walk into the lush springtime woods, crouch among some bushes, and his father would squawk on his crow call. "I'm in trouble," was his message. A long, plaintive caw on the call, followed by two shorter caws, then a pause, and then the same call repeated, this time with more urgency to it. "Come help me," his old man was pleading to the flock.

First they'd hear the distant, worried chattering of the crows discussing the situation. Then the scout would come, flying low and fast and silent, and from where Nick was hiding he could sometimes see the scout's glittery intelligent eyes checking everything out, scanning the underbrush, looking for the lost baby. Crows had powerful family instincts and a highly evolved social structure. When one crow was in trouble, it concerned all of them.

Nick liked crows. They were very civilized and cooperative. They raided songbird and duck nests, he knew. But they never killed each other.

When the scout came, Nick and his father had two options. They could shoot the scout. Then the rest of the flock would come to find out what had happened to it. Or they could remain hidden, and if the scout didn't see them, it would perch in a nearby tree and call to the rest of the flock to come help.

Heartbreak 1963

191

But if they shot and missed, or if the scout spotted them, it would swoop away with a staccato *caw-caw-caw* that, Nick had learned, meant: "Stay away! There's two guys here, and they've got shotguns!"

Crows were cautious and clever, worthy quarry for a hunter. Nick liked trying to call them in. But after his father died, he had stopped trying to shoot them. He'd decided he admired them too much.

He hadn't come to Heartbreak to hunt crows on this cold Monday in November. He wasn't sure he'd hunt at all. But it had been a year and two months since his father died, and then there had been the long weekend, holed up alone in his apartment listening to the hushed, somber voices of Chet and David, and Nick had to get away from all of it.

He had seen skim ice along the edges of the pond when he'd left his apartment in the morning. Soon the inland creeks and swamps would be frozen. Then the black ducks would come to Heartbreak, and Nick would walk the marsh at dawn when the sky was purple and a blush of pink was just beginning to color the horizon. He'd sneak up on the tidal creeks and gullies and potholes the way he used to with his father. He'd go down on elbows and knees for the last fifty feet, and when he poked his head over the bank, the ducks would burst into the air.

Upland Days

192

His father had loved jump-shooting black ducks here. Nick wished he knew why the old man had called it Heartbreak.

When he was just a boy, too young to carry a gun, Nick had followed behind his father, creeping over the brittle brown marsh grass and frozen mud. It had crunched under their boots, as if they were walking on Wheaties. Sometimes they heard the muffled gabble of ducks in the potholes somewhere ahead of them. Then the old man would hold up his hand for Nick to stop, and he'd point with his finger. Nick's father had known every pothole and creek-corner on Heartbreak. He'd always known where the ducks would be. He'd known a lot of things. When he died, everything he'd known was lost.

One morning when Nick was twelve, they'd crept right up to the edge of a creek bank. It was low tide, so the ducks were down low and hadn't seen them. The old man had turned and pressed his Model 21 into Nick's hands. "You take 'em, Nicholas," he had whispered.

Nick eased to the side, and when his father gave the signal they both stood up. A dozen ducks jumped straight up off the water. The shotgun came up to Nick's shoulder, and he remembered to flick off the safety with his thumb. He mounted one of those big birds on top of the barrels and pulled the trigger. The

Heartbreak 1963

bird hesitated, then tipped to the side with only one wing still flapping. Nick shot it again, and it somersaulted into the water.

Nick had always shot the Model 21 well.

His old man had died of stomach cancer. He wasn't that old. About the same age as the man who'd died in Dallas. It had taken Nick's old man a long time to die, and toward the end he'd cried from the pain and didn't recognize anybody. It had frightened Nick to see his father cry, and it made him angry, too. A bullet in the head was a much better way, Nick had thought at the time. Now he wasn't so sure.

The coffee had gone cold in the steel cup and Nick's legs were stiff from sitting there with his back against the dead tree. He stood up and stretched and looked at the ridgeline. The crows weren't there anymore. He hadn't noticed when they'd left.

He fished two shells from the pocket of his hunting vest and slipped them into the shotgun. Then he closed it, lifting the stock to meet the barrels the way his father had taught him. It shut with the good click of a well-made piece of machinery, like the doors of a Cadillac.

He headed across the meadow toward the low wooded hills that sloped down to the Heartbreak marsh. The goldenrod and

Upland Days

194

thick grass where he and his father had sometimes found pheasants were frost-killed and wind-flattened, and Nick walked briskly. He carried the shotgun at his side. Without a dog, he knew he wouldn't get a shot. Any pheasants in the meadow would flush wild and fly into the woods or run ahead and crouch in the briar tangles along the edge.

His father had told him that ruffed grouse used to live in those woods. Back when the old man was Nick's age, the Heartbreak woods had grown thick with wild apple, birch saplings, scrub oak, alder, hemlock, and young poplar. His old man had called it popple. But over the years, the trees had grown tall, and their shade had killed the underbrush and weeds on the forest floor, and Nick's father said there were no more grouse, which he called partridge.

Nick didn't really care whether he found any birds. He just had to get away from the television for a day. If he'd stayed home, he knew he would've kept it on and thought about his old man.

By the time he had crossed the meadow, he was sweating under his heavy wool shirt and hunting vest. He paused to peer into the woods. They were silent and shadowy and lifeless there on the shaded side of the hill. He considered turning around and walking back. But all he had to go back to was his empty apartment and his black-and-white television.

Heartbreak 1963

195

So he followed along the thick edge where the meadow met the woods. He moved slowly, pausing now and then to kick at a blowdown or a clump of brush. His father had taught him how wild birds will sit still as long as they know where you are. They can hear you no matter how quiet you are, he had said. They survive because they always know where their predators are. You can't be as quiet as a fox or a hawk, Nicholas, so there's no sense in trying to sneak up on them. When you stop and stand still, they lose track of you. Then they panic and take flight. The trick, Nick's father always said, was to move steadily, then stop in a place that would give you a good shot. That's when the birds would fly.

Nick moved along the edge of the woods for a mile or so, stopping now and then the way his father had taught him. He flushed nothing and realized he didn't have much heart for hunting today. So he pushed through the brush into the dark woods and turned around to head back.

He'd gone a hundred yards or so when he crossed a stone wall and came upon an old cellar hole. The fieldstone chimney had toppled into it, and at the bottom, all tangled in briars and frost-killed milkweed, were old charred timbers and rusted bedsprings. Tall oak trees now met in a leafless canopy overhead, but Nick could visualize how it had once been, this farmer's house sitting in the opening he'd cleared on the edge of his pasture with the

Upland Days

196

Heartbreak marsh in the distance, and beyond it the ocean where the sun rose in a blush of pink every morning. Old lilac bushes, grown into tall spindly trees now, stood at each corner of the cellar hole.

A little farther on Nick found the family burying ground. The gravestones were toppled and cracked and half covered with dead weeds. A century of rain and ice and wind had scoured their faces so that Nick couldn't read the words and numbers that had been scratched into them.

Moving beyond the graveyard, he crossed another stone wall and came to a stand of barren old fruit trees. They were stunted and gnarly and gray, and they looked like runts next to the tall pines that grew among them. But Nick could see how they had been planted in neat rows, the same way the stone walls had been laid out, and Nick thought about the old farmer who had done all that work. His stone walls and family grave markers and his cellar hole were all still here, though he was long gone, and that reminded him of his father, who had been precise about everything. He had always worked hard and was gone now, too.

The grouse flushed from nearly under his feet. Then two more birds burst away a little farther ahead. Their explosive flushes were as unexpected and startling as those sniper's bullets

Heartbreak 1963

197

in Dallas, but Nick's shotgun—his father's old Model 21—came up to his shoulder on its own. His thumb flicked off the safety, and he mounted the nearest of the gray birds over his gun barrels and pulled the trigger without any conscious thought whatsoever.

He didn't see the grouse come down, but he heard its rapid flurry of wingbeats drumming on the hard ground under the old apple trees.

By the time Nick found it, the bird's wings had stopped drumming. He picked it up, cradled it in his palm, and stroked its breast feathers and the little crest on its head with his forefinger. The bird's neck drooped limply from his hand, and a drop of blood slowly formed on the tip of its beak and dropped onto Nick's boot.

His father had said there were no more ruffed grouse in these woods. It was the first time Nick could remember that his father had been wrong.

He stuffed the grouse into the back of his hunting vest. He kept his shotgun broken open as he walked back to his car.

By the time he got there, the afternoon shadows were long and the sun was sinking behind the hills. He took the bird from his game pocket, smoothed down its feathers, and laid it gently

Upland Days

on the floor behind the front seat. He wondered why he didn't feel that little twinge of regret and sadness that he usually felt when he shot something.

But he didn't feel sad. In fact, he realized he felt better than he'd felt in a year and two months. He didn't understand why, but he knew it was something he'd think about and figure out eventually.

Nick listened to the funeral on the car radio on the way back to his apartment. The priest's voice was hesitant and mournful, and by the time he finished his eulogy, saying, "Good-bye, dear Jack," Nick's eyes were burning. He guessed it was about time he cried for his father.

The funeral drums were muffled and slow, much slower than the wingbeats of his grouse when they'd drummed on the frozen ground under that old farmer's apple trees in the Heartbreak woods.

Chapter 17

November Flight

October 1, Opening Day. Indian summer in Maine. The maples and poplars still clung to their leaves, the kind of flashy crimson-and-gold foliage that delights leaf-peepers with cameras but makes woodcock shooting with 20-gauge shotguns just about impossible. By mid-morning, the temperature had pushed into the 80s. Down by the brook at the far end of Stick Farm, where a resident woodcock or two always lived, the ground was baked hard. We found no birds there, or on John's Knoll, either. Keith did spot some dried-up chalking in Arnold's Pasture. But no birds. A grouse flushed wild out of a pine tree at County Line. And that was our morning hunt.

Upland Days

200

After lunch, Burt, my Brittany pup, flash-pointed and then busted a single woodcock from the alders behind the Hippie House. He gave chase. We heard the twitter of wings, but never saw the bird through the leaves.

When Burt came prancing back, I gave him hell. But my heart wasn't in it. It had been nearly a year since he'd whiffed a woodcock, and our dust-dry covers weren't giving him many birdy smells on this opening day.

We saved Five Aces for last, according to our tradition. It was Freebie's turn for her first—and only—hunt of the day.

This was the fourteenth season for Keith's old dog. She was a pointer-setter dropper, an accident, according to her original owner, who'd been happy to foist her off on Keith. She'd cost Keith nothing. A Freebie.

She staggered for a moment when he lifted her down from the truck. He shoved three aspirins into the back of her mouth, then held her jaws shut and stroked her throat to make her swallow.

She limped into the alders, the portrait of an eager spirit but a reluctant body, and I knew Keith was remembering what I remembered—how she used to prance and glide, tail and head held high, and how she would quarter a woodcock cover, cutting it into systematic slices, and how Keith never had to whistle her

November Flight

in, because when her bell fell silent it meant she was pointing, and we could trust her to hold it until we found her, no matter how long it took.

Freebie was one helluva bird dog.

We lost sight of her in the leafy thicket almost immediately. We loaded our shotguns and stepped into the cover.

Freebie's bell had stopped. "Over here," called Keith matter-of-factly. "The old gal's got one pinned."

It was a classic Freebie point—tail ramrod straight, body canted forward, ears cocked, eyes intent, nose aquiver—although I did notice a slight tremble in her legs.

Keith and I moved forward. But when the woodcock flushed, neither of us saw it through the leaves.

Five minutes later, Freebie lay down and couldn't get up. Keith carried her back to the car, leaving the prime cuts of Five Aces unexplored.

It had been a long, cold, wet spring up and down the East Coast, the worst possible nesting conditions for woodcock. And the data from the annual singing-ground counts were again ominous. Woodcock numbers had been plummeting for two decades.

Upland Days

202

We knew the old days were gone, those glorious October mornings when young Freebie would trot purposefully from point to point and even mediocre wingshots like Keith and me sometimes bagged our limits in the day's the first cover. We'd lost several of those good old woodcock covers to houses and industrial parks and highways and No Hunting signs, but most of them had simply petered out—gradually surrendering their birdy edges to the encroachments of maturing forest.

Still, in a lifetime of up-and-down woodcock seasons, this one promised to be the most discouraging. After that Opening Day, we waited a week. But still the New England line storm did not come to rip the leaves from the saplings and fill the brooks, and no killing frost flattened the goldenrod and softened the fallen apples.

We tried it a week after Opening Day and quit at noon, sweaty and discouraged, without firing a shot. Keith didn't bother to let Freebie out of the car.

Two days of wind and rain in the third week of the season tore the leaves from the trees, and then several nights of heavy frost turned the landscape brown. Our covers finally started to look birdy. The woodcock flights were overdue, and we hunted every morning.

November Flight

Maybe if Freebie had been healthy, if she'd been able to quarter through the woods all day the way she once could, we'd have had some shooting. But after ten or fifteen minutes of hunting, she'd collapse, struggle to rise, then give up, and Keith would lug her back to the car.

Burt hunted enthusiastically, but there just weren't enough gamy smells to keep his attention. He chased stink birds and followed deer scent. Once he pointed a porcupine, another time a pile of steaming moose scat.

And then, too soon, it was November and the final two days of the woodcock season were upon us.

Keith and I met at the stone bridge at nine o'clock, as we always did, and we leaned against our cars to sip coffee and lay plans, the way we'd been doing for nearly twenty years.

Keith squinted up at the gray sky. A cold mist was falling, and the air felt still and heavy. "Got me a thought," he said.

"Good," I said. "Myself, I'm plumb out of thoughts."

"Let's fool 'em. Do it backwards. Hit Five Aces first. Cool day like this, maybe Freebie can make it all the way through. I'd sure like to give her a shot at it."

"Suits me," I said.

Upland Days

204

We'd found Five Aces on a topographic map one winter afternoon more than a decade earlier, when Freebie was still a pup—the square of an old cellar hole, the meandering dotted line of a dirt road, the thin blue line of a brook tracing the curve along the bottom of a hillside. When we checked it out the following October, it looked as good as it had on the map. The pastures had grown up to mingled clumps of old Baldwin apple and juniper and birch. The sunny hillside stood thick with poplar and birch saplings and sloped down to a boggy brook bordered by alder. When we followed the brook, we stumbled onto a hidden swamp, and on that first day we found it full of woodcock.

Keith had shot two grouse and three woodcock with five shells that first day we hunted there—all over Freebie's points. I wanted to call our new cover "Keith's Fluke." He favored "Tap's Folly," to commemorate the fact that I'd shot more times than he had without touching a feather.

"Five Aces" was our compromise. Over the years, it had been our most dependable cover, our ace in the hole, and even though it had been on the decline in recent years, that was relative. All of our covers had been declining. Five Aces usually held more birds, and always more memories, than any of the others.

November Flight

Keith fed Freebie her aspirins, and she hobbled into the woods. Then her bell stopped. "What a dog," murmured Keith. "We got a point. Let's go."

She had a grouse cornered under an apple tree, and Keith missed it with both barrels.

We hunted the pasture and the hillside, and although we found no more birds, Freebie kept going—not fast, and not with that old cocky verve, but she was hunting, quartering through the woods, turning now and then to make sure we were doing it right.

We reconnoitered at the top of the hillside. Keith sighed. "I really did have a feeling," he said. "Thought sure we'd find woodcock today. They gotta come down sometime."

"We've still got the hidden swamp."

"Dunno," he said. "Not sure I'm up for lugging Freebie all the way back to the truck from there."

"Remember that first day, when we discovered the swamp?"

"There must've been two dozen woodcock in there."

I nodded. "We'll never know unless we take a look."

"Okay." He smiled. "But you gotta carry her halfway."

"I would be honored," I said.

Upland Days

206

The swamp was peppered with spring seeps, and a step-over brook snaked through the middle of it. The earth was black and boggy under its thin blanket of fallen leaves, and the alders and scrubby pines grew in islands.

Freebie locked on a point almost immediately. Keith and I moved in, and the woodcock spurted up from my feet. My shotgun came up, and I muttered, "Wait on him," before I fired. Still too quick, but I dropped it with the second barrel. Freebie limped over, picked up the bird, and carried it to Keith, who handed it to me.

I stroked the woodcock's feathers, then slid it into my game pocket. "Well, all right," I said. It was the first woodcock either of us had shot the entire season.

"There's chalking everywhere," said Keith. "Looks like the flights are finally in. Where's Freebie?"

She was pointing. Keith kicked up the bird, and as he dropped it, two more twittered up. One crossed in front of me and I knocked it down. I heard Keith shoot again.

A minute later Freebie had deposited three woodcock in Keith's hand.

"Got me another thought," said Keith.

November Flight

"So far your thoughts've been pretty good," I said. "Let's hear it."

"We got ourselves two brace of woodcock," he said quietly, "which is as much as any gentleman ought to take in a day." He arched his eyebrows.

I nodded. "Swamp's full of birds. Let's not jostle the rest of 'em. Tomorrow's the last day of the season. We'll come back, have ourselves a time."

"That was my thought, precisely."

So we turned our backs on the hidden swamp and headed up the hill. Freebie heeled for a few minutes, then lay down. Keith and I took turns carrying her out.

I didn't sleep well that night, reliving Freebie's points, the whistle of wings, the hidden swamp in Five Aces white with woodcock splashing and bursting with birds, everything just the way I remembered it.

When Keith lifted Freebie from the truck at Five Aces the next morning, her legs splayed out. She tried to stand, but couldn't lift her hindquarters.

So we brought Burt. He quartered the cover like a veteran, cutting it into slices, checking back to be sure Keith and I were doing it right, carrying his head and stubby little tail high, doing it the way he'd seen Freebie do it.

But we didn't find a single woodcock in the hidden swamp.

Back at the truck, Keith laughed. "Well, that's woodcock for you," he said. "They've pushed on, and that's that."

"Guess we should've shot our limits yesterday," I said, "when we had the chance."

"No," he said. "We did it just right."

Keith called me the day after Thanksgiving. "Took Freebie to the vet this morning," he said. "Held her head on my lap while he put her down."

"I'm sorry, old friend," was all I could think of to say.

"Don't be," he said. "I know she was remembering that morning in the hidden swamp. Her last hunt. She was still smelling those woodcock when she closed her eyes."

Chapter 18

Hunting for Burt

The Town Line Cover rambles around a big flat hilltop somewhere in the northwestern corner of New Hampshire.

It's a three-hour drive from my home to the gas station/six-pack/nightcrawler store, where Keith and I meet. Then we follow several dirt roads, taking the least-traveled fork every time there's an option. The last one is more mud and granite ledge than dirt, and even with Keith's four-wheel-drive truck, we're never confident we'll get back out.

Three or four dairy farms occupied this hilltop a century ago. The caved-in cellar holes are still there, and big leggy lilacs and clusters of gnarly old apple and pear trees grow in the dooryards. Meandering stone walls mark the boundaries of the ancient pas-

Upland Days

210

tures. I always wonder if those flinty old Yankees appreciated the view of the White Mountains from their hilltop. I suspect they worked too hard trying to stay alive to even notice.

The forests have been harvested periodically by loggers in the years since the old farmers abandoned their land. The woodcutters hacked mazes of new roads into the woods, and then logged the areas near the roads. Even today there's some cutting going on, and someone mows the fields and cuts the brush out of the roads every few years.

All this haphazard clearing, abandoning, growing, cutting, and regenerating has created a patchwork of fields, stands of young second-growth softwood, brushy edges, ancient orchards, thick screens of pine, and mature oak and maple forests, all intersected by tote roads and stone walls and step-over brooks. There are alder runs and poplar hillsides and grapevine tangles. Old pastures grow waist-high in goldenrod and milkweed and are studded with juniper and thornapple and clumps of apple and hemlock and briar. Here and there a spring-fed trout stream follows the creases in the earth. The inevitable beaver ponds harbor wood ducks and native brookies. The beavers are doing their part to keep the land cleared.

Hunting for Burt

In other words, the Town Line Cover is classic grouse and woodcock habitat, and it's worth the long drive it takes to get there and the full day it takes to hunt it properly. I don't think there are many other places left in New England quite like it.

On this bright morning in late October, we find the leaves still clinging stubbornly to the trees, and the air is soft and unseasonably warm. But there's dew on the grass, and we had hard rain a few days earlier. The ground is spongy, the scenting conditions are perfect, and we've heard that the woodcock flights are in.

Keith and I follow the edges of a tongue of thick cover that divides two old pastures. Burt works the tangly stuff between us. Usually he's wild and heedless in the day's first cover, but he worked hard yesterday, got his edge taken off, and this morning he zigzags back and forth, always within sight of either Keith or me.

Suddenly Burt stops, hesitates, begins tiptoeing. His stubby tail is a blur. "He's birdy," I call to Keith. "Be ready."

A moment later, the grouse spurts noisily but unseen out of the tip of the thicket, far ahead of us. Burt hears it, raises his head, thinks about giving chase, then returns to business.

Upland Days

212

We cross a field to a slope just starting to grow back to poplar and birch. The young trees are no more than ten or twelve feet tall. "Reminds me of Stick Farm," says Keith. Stick Farm used to be one of our most dependable covers in Maine. In recent years it's disappointed us. "The way it used to look, I mean," he adds.

Burt locks on point barely fifteen feet into the cover. Keith moves along the roadway on the left. I remain standing at the field edge. "You clear for a shot?" I call to Keith.

"Depends on which way he flies."

"Don't it always."

I shoulder my way into the thick cover. Burt's nose is quivering. Another step, and the woodcock flushes. My gun comes up, but the bird is flying low, heading Keith's way.

He shoots. Both barrels. They sound like misses.

Then a second woodcock whistles up and angles away to my right. By the time I swing in its direction, it's just a flicker in the leaves. I shoot at the flicker. Then I see the bird above the treetops, flying hard, already out of range.

"Well?" I call.

"Nope. You?"

"Me, neither."

Hunting for Burt

Four other woodcock have settled into this two-acre patch of poplar. Burt points each of them. Keith and I miss them all.

Time to reconnoiter.

I sit on a stump. Keith perches on the stone wall. We discuss strategy. Should we follow that last woodcock? Keith got a good line on it. Or maybe we should hook around and work back along the far side of the cover. I think one of those birds might've come down there, and we never did hunt that edge.

Keith is rummaging in the pocket of his hunting vest. "At this rate I'm gonna run out of shells," he grumbles. Then he laughs. "You notice anything peculiar?"

"Aside from the fact that Burt pointed every woodcock in there?"

Keith gives Burt's forehead a scratch. "He keeps that up, we'll forget Freebie."

"We'll never forget Freebie," I say. "What'm I supposed to notice?"

"How many shots did you take in there?"

I shrug. "Not sure. Guess I wasted five shells. Maybe six."

"Me, too," he says.

"Well, hell," I say. "That's not worth noticing."

"So what's your excuse?"

Upland Days

"Me?" I shrug. "Poor shooting, I guess."

"What about the foliage? Kinda thick for good shooting. Wasn't the sun in your eyes or something?"

"Nah. Lousy shooting, that's all."

He nods. "Exactly my point. No excuses. No complaints. I remember when you'd cuss and scream whenever you missed, which was quite often, as I recall."

"So did you."

"Sure I did. So what's the matter with us?"

"Matter?" I say. "Nothing. I'm having a pretty good time, myself."

"Precisely," says Keith. "A bunch of easy chances, not a feather in my pocket, and I'm sitting here thinking, 'Hey, this is perfect.'"

"Well, it's damn close to perfect. Except I'd like to reward Burt's points now and then with a dead bird, just to remind him of what it's all about."

Keith arches his eyebrows at me. "So what *is* it all about?"

Right now, Burt's in his prime. He's five years old—young and strong and sharp-nosed and eager. He can run all day—usually too hard and too fast in the morning's first cover, when his en-

Hunting for Burt

thusiasm and his field-trial genes overpower his training. He's always got to bust a bird or two before he remembers that he can't catch them. Then he settles down and starts hunting.

I wish he'd hunt closer, but he was bred to range wide, and I've given up trying to keep him reined in. I let him gallop for the first fifteen minutes or so—preferably not in one of our good covers—because I know he'll get it out of his system and spend the rest of the day hunting with me. He never ranges beyond the sound of his bell, so when I stop hearing it, I trust that he's on point. In the thick early-season woods, it sometimes takes a while to track him down.

He'll hold a point as long as the bird will sit. I've spent a lot of time hunting for Burt in the woods.

When I started bird hunting as a teenager, there were plenty of farms and second-growth woodlots right in my hometown where I could reasonably expect to find a pheasant or a few grouse or a pod of woodcock. I could walk out the back door of my home in eastern Massachusetts, load my shotgun, stride into the woods out back, and go hunting.

Gradually the farms in my hometown became housing developments, and my search for birdy places led me farther and far-

Upland Days

ther from home—first to nearby towns, then to Spiller country in southern New Hampshire, then to central New Hampshire, then to Keith's string of covers in west-central Maine. Each area produced for a while, then seemed to peter out.

In recent years, I've had to do a lot of driving to find productive covers. Even the best of them generally don't look as good as those I remember, and when I get there, they usually hold fewer birds. There are no more spur-of-the-moment grouse and woodcock trips. No longer can I look out the window, feel that old itch, grab my shotgun and a box of shells, whistle up the dog, and spend a couple of afternoon hours in the woods. These days, an upland hunting trip is . . . a trip. It takes planning and coordinating. Where do we meet? Where will we sleep? Who'll bring the food? Who knows some good places to hunt?

The fact is, nowadays it takes a real effort to go hunting. Maybe I'm just growing old and lazy. It's possible, though I'm not quite ready to admit it. I do know that the scarcity of grouse and the frightening decline in woodcock numbers have dampened my enthusiasm for killing them.

For a while there, a few years back, entire October and November weekends came and went and my shotgun stayed in its case. I left it up to Keith and Skip and Art and other friends

Hunting for Burt

who owned bird dogs to invite me to hunt with them, and when no one called, I didn't go.

When I didn't go, I missed it. Driving past an autumn field bordering an overgrown orchard, or a golden hillside sprouting head-high poplar and birch, or a meandering valley of alder along a woodland brook—those sights never failed to stir old longings. But not hunting did not burn a hole in my stomach. I had plenty of good memories—maybe a lifetime's worth. They sustained me through those October and November New England weekends when I stayed home, and a few outings a season were enough to keep me going for another year.

When I thought about it, it worried me. I'd seen it happen to men of my father's generation. The loss of the hunting urge seemed, in them, like the natural progression of things. Their dogs got old. So did they. Their fires died. Hunting, they said, was too strenuous, took too much energy, left them too lame the next day. Anyway, they'd already shot a lifetime's worth of birds, and it wasn't anything like the good old days, when a man couldn't possibly feel guilty about harvesting a limit of grouse or woodcock.

I could never figure out if this was their rationalization, and if it was, what exactly they were trying to rationalize. But when I

Upland Days

felt it beginning to happen to me, it just seemed as if some vital element in my soul was slowly bleeding away, the way, I'm told, the sex drive or the burning need to get rich eventually dries up. When it's gone, you don't even miss it.

I still liked to hunt. But I was beginning to understand that I could live without it.

It's entirely possible, in fact, that I might have gradually arrived at the point where I stopped hunting altogether, not because I'd weighed the costs and benefits of hunting and found the costs too high, but simply out of inertia.

Then, five years ago, Burt joined the family.

He was a Brittany, a surprise birthday gift from Vicki, eight weeks old and about ten pounds of sniff and wiggle. I named him "Burton Spiller's Firelight," after my old friend.

He sight-pointed a moth the July afternoon that I brought him home. He was pointing the pheasant wing I'd strung from the tip of an old fly rod before he was housebroken. That first summer, Burt pointed the quail that Marty Connolly scattered in the weeds for him, and I held him steady to wing on a check cord. I tried to train him according to the books. It wasn't hard. He quickly learned to come, to heel, to whoa, to sit, to stay. The

Hunting for Burt

normal command—"Kennel"—he and I modified to "Get-in-the-car."

By September, I was eager for the hunting season—more eager, I realized, than I'd been for years. I couldn't wait to see how Burt would handle wild birds.

When the first of October rolled around, Burt was two weeks shy of five months old. He was about the size of a long-legged beagle. Just a pup.

My hunting log for that season reminds me that we hunted with Keith and Freebie on Opening Day. We found the woods tinder-dry. The leaves had barely started to turn, and the trees had not started to drop them. The woodcock flights had not arrived. We bumped just three—and no grouse—from our good covers, shot none, and got no points, even from the veteran Freebie. Burt snuffled around. He seemed to ignore Freebie, though I had the feeling he was watching the old dog out of the corner of his eye. He appeared to be hunting. He obeyed my commands well enough. But as far as I could tell, he never got a whiff of a woodcock.

Art Currier and I hunted with Marty Connolly the following Saturday. Marty promised he could show Burt where some woodcock were hiding, and he was as good as his word. Burt's first woodcock points came that day, and that was when he introduced me to his version of retrieving. First he pointed a dead bird that had landed in a juniper. The second bird we shot he found, flash-pointed, thought better of it, and stood over it protectively until he knew I could find it. Then he wandered off to find another.

A little later, when Art wing-tipped a woodcock, Burt pinned it gently to the ground with his paw until I picked it up.

A few days later we hunted with Skip Rood and Waldo, Skip's wily old Brittany. Waldo was a legend. Those who'd hunted with him called him "Waldo the Wonder Dog." He was fourteen years old and stone-deaf. But his nose was still sharp, and his instincts were well honed by his years of experience. I figured Burt could learn something from Waldo, as he'd seemed to from Freebie.

The first cover we hunted that day bordered a pond. Burt and I followed the ridgeline, while Skip and Waldo worked the edge of the pond below us. Five minutes into the cover, Skip said conversationally, "Waldo's got a point." A moment later I heard his 28-gauge double bark once. Then: "Dammit!"

"Miss him?" I called.

"Worse. Dropped him in the middle of the pond."

Hunting for Burt

Arthritic old Waldo, I knew, would not, could not, retrieve a bird from the water. I wondered if Skip was prepared to swim for it. I sure wasn't.

"Need some help?" I yelled.

"Dunno what we can do... wait... Burt's swimming out there... I'll be damned."

I hurried down to the pond and got to the bank in time to see Burt, a good forty yards out in the pond, nudging a dead, floating grouse with his nose. The bird looked as big as he was, but somehow he got his mouth around it and paddled back to shore.

He dropped the grouse on the ground at my feet, shook the water out of his fur, and went back to looking for birds.

I hunted as often as I could that first season. I hunted more than I had in the previous four or five seasons combined—every weekend plus a couple of weekday afternoons each week. When the season ended, I took Burt to some private hunting preserves. I wanted to fill his nose with bird smells and to fill the air with rocketing game birds and the sounds of shotguns and the smell of gunpowder.

And thus it has been since Burt came into my life. We hunt hard in the fall. In the spring, we hunt—without shotguns—for

Upland Days

migrating woodcock that he can point. We hunt, or we practice hunting, all year round.

Maybe I've reached the point in my life when I don't need to hunt. But I have accepted an obligation. I owe hunting to Burt. It's what he lives for. Hunting drives him and fulfills him. Poets must write, artists must paint, and bird dogs must hunt.

Yes, I hunt because my father hunted, and my father's father before him, and for all those other complicated psychological and cultural and genetic and personal reasons. But these days, more than anything, I hunt for Burt.

We are working our way down an alder-studded slope when Burt points again. I whistle to Keith, wait for him to get into position for a shot, then step in front of Burt.

The woodcock rises from under his nose and beats its way straight up to the top of the thick alders. I shoot without thinking, and the bird crumples and falls.

"Git 'im?" calls Keith.

"Yep."

" 'Bout time."

I find Burt standing over the dead bird. I pick it up, smooth its feathers, and hold it down for Burt, who gives it a cursory sniff and wanders away.

Hunting for Burt

223

Keith comes over, and we break our guns and sit on a log.

"A ways back there," I say, "you were asking what it's all about. How we could enjoy ourselves hunting when we weren't shooting a damn thing."

"Rhetorical question. The great mystery of life."

"It's a significantly lesser mystery," I say. "But I think I've figured it out."

"I'm not sure I want to know," he says. "I like mysteries."

"Tough. Listen. In the beginning, men trained and bred dogs to hunt for them. Hounds to chase, terriers to dig, flushers to flush, pointers to point, retrievers to retrieve. The dogs' job was to find game so men could kill it and bring it home to eat. You with me so far?"

Keith smiles.

"So," I continue, "Burt's job is to hunt for me. To sniff up birds and go point them, so I can kick them up and shoot them." I poke Keith's arm. "Remember how Freebie always pointed a woodcock in that corner right over the stone wall at Stick Farm, and how you got such a kick out of predicting it?"

"She was something, all right," says Keith softly.

"How would you have felt about walking into that corner without Freebie and kicking up that woodcock and shooting it?"

Upland Days

He shrugs. "Wouldn't've bothered doing that. No point to it." He chuckles. "Pun intended."

"Exactly," I say. "So Freebie might've been trying to find birds for us, but—"

"But," he says, "the fact is, we were trying to find birds for her. It's a fact. When I went hunting, it was as much for Freebie as it was for me."

"So that's it. That's what it's all about. That's why shooting and missing really doesn't bother me anymore. Burt doesn't seem to care one way or the other, as long as he gets to point them. And if he doesn't care, I don't, either. Now when I hunt, it's for Burt."

Keith cups his hand around his ear. "Speaking of hunting for Burt," he says, "I don't hear his bell."

I listen. The woods are silent. I stand up, pick up my shotgun, and slide in two shells. "Let's go," I say. "I believe we got ourselves another point."